Jasmine
and Coconuts

World Folklore Advisory Board

Jasmine and Coconuts

South Indian Tales

Cathy Spagnoli

and

Paramasivam Samanna

Illustrated by
Paramasivam Samanna

1999
Libraries Unlimited, Inc.
Englewood, Colorado

Libraries Unlimited, Inc.
P.O. Box 6633
Englewood, CO 80155-6633
1-800-237-6124
www.lu.com

Production Editor: Kevin W. Perizzolo
Copy Editor: D. Aviva Rothschild
Proofreader: Eileen Bartlett
Indexer: Christine Smith
Typesetter: Kay Minnis

Library of Congress Cataloging-in-Publication Data

Spagnoli, Cathy.
    Jasmine and coconuts : South Indian tales / Cathy Spagnoli and Paramasivam Samanna.
    xvi, 182 p. 19x26 cm. -- (World folklore series)
    Includes bibliographical references and index.
    ISBN 1-56308-576-3 (hc.)
    1. Tales--India--Tamil Nadu. 2. Tamil (Indic people)--Folklore.
3. Folk literature, Tamil--History and criticism. 4. India--
History--Study and teaching. I. Samanna, Paramasivam. II. Title.
III. Series.
GR305.5.T3S63   1998
398.2'0954'82—dc21
                                                        98-36548
                                                           CIP

In memory of Gene Spagnoli

who so inspired us,

but too soon left us

Temple elephant from Tirupati, Andhra Pradesh.
Photo courtesy of Rajani Bommakanti.

World Folklore Series

1991 Folk Stories of the Hmong: Peoples of Laos, Thailand, and Vietnam. By Norma J. Livo and Dia Cha.

1992 Images of a People: Tlingit Myths and Legends. By Mary Helen Pelton and Jacqueline DiGennaro.

1994 Hyena and the Moon: Stories to Tell from Kenya. By Heather McNeil.

1994 The Corn Woman: Stories and Legends of the Hispanic Southwest. Retold by Angel Vigil. Translated by Juan Francisco Marín and Jennifer Audrey Lowell.

1994 Thai Tales: Folktales of Thailand. Retold by Supaporn Vathanaprida. Edited by Margaret Read MacDonald.

1996 In Days Gone By: Folklore and Traditions of the Pennsylvania Dutch. By Audrey Burie Kirchner and Margaret R. Tassia.

1997 From the Mango Tree and Other Folktales from Nepal. By Kavita Ram Shrestha and Sarah Lamstein.

1997 Why Ostriches Don't Fly and Other Tales from the African Bush. By I. Murphy Lewis.

1997 The Magic Egg and Other Tales from Ukraine. Retold by Barbara J. Suwyn. Edited and with an Introduction by Natalie O. Kononenko.

1999 Jasmine and Coconuts: South Indian Tales. By Cathy Spagnoli and Paramasivam Samanna.

1999 When Night Falls, Kric! Krac! Haitian Folktales. By Liliane Nérette Louis. Edited by Fred Hay, Ph.D.

1999 A Tiger by the Tail and Other Stories from the Heart of Korea. By Lindy Soon Curry. Edited by Chan-eung Park.

1999 The Enchanted Wood and Other Tales from Finland. By Norma J. Livo and George O. Livo.

Selections Available on Audiocassette

1995 Hyena and the Moon: Stories to Listen to from Kenya. By Heather McNeil.

1995 The Corn Woman: Audio Stories and Legends of the Hispanic Southwest. English and Spanish versions. By Angel Vigil. Spanish version read by Juan Francisco Marín.

1997 Thai Tales: Audio Folktales from Thailand. By Supaporn Vathanaprida and Margaret Read MacDonald. Narrated by Supaporn Vathanaprida. Produced and with an Introduction by Margaret Read MacDonald.

1998 Folk Stories of the Hmong: Audio Tales from the Peoples of Laos, Thailand, and Vietnam. By Norma J. Livo and Dia Cha. Narrated by Norma J. Livo and Dia Cha.

Contents

Preface

We had been gathering the stories in this book long before we started writing it. Paramasivam grew up in Tamil Nadu, South India, hearing proverbs and tales. And over the years, I have slipped through rice fields, sat through all-night story sessions, and walked on long pilgrimages seeking stories and meeting wonderful South Indian storytellers.

This book began as a simple collection of stories but soon grew out of hand. There are so many groups, beliefs, and stories in South India that it was almost impossible to choose a story selection that included everything and pleased everyone. It was also important, yet difficult, to write background cultural material and to find photographs that truly reflected the rich diversity of the lesser-known south of India. A good friend from Kerala, L. S. Rajagopalan, wrote that we seemed to be trying not only to swallow a large pestle, but to swallow it horizontally!

We did what we could. We squeezed tales from Paramasivam's memory, pored over my journals, and even sent questionnaires to South Indian friends here and abroad. We then faced large problems in editing and in spelling out words from the four different southern languages, words that are transliterated in many varied ways. Because our book is primarily for use in schools and libraries, we decided to avoid often confusing diacritical marks and to write out words as simply as possible, with commonly used English spellings for many of the names, like the *Ramayana*. We have also followed the frequent practice of dividing words to make them easier to pronounce: Tamil Nadu instead of Tamilnadu.

Place-names were a challenge as well, for some Indian states are now using regional language names to replace British forms (e.g., Chennai for Madras). These changes are not always widely accepted, but we use them in respect, placing the former names in brackets at first. Finally, we have used B.C.E. (before the common era) as a more neutral abbreviation than B.C., as well as C.E. (common era) for A.D. when needed.

The oil lamp is lit for worship and for special occasions.

We wish to thank all of the Indian tellers and friends who have been so gracious over the years. As a small gesture in their honor, half of the royalties from this book will go to fund self-help, rural development projects in India through a fine nonprofit group, People for Progress in India.

In the text, credit is given as needed. Thus, if a quotation appears without a source, it comes from my journals or interviews. The photographs are from Sangeet Natak Akademi in India, the government body that supports and documents performing arts; Lou Corbett; Raghavendra Rao; Rajani Bommakanti; A. D. Edward Raj; and our own collection. Any blame for oversights and mistakes in the book should fall on us, while any credit must be shared with all of the wonderful people who have helped us, including, but not limited to, those on this list.

CATHY SPAGNOLI

Our parents, our extended families, and our son Manu

The great folks at Vashon Library, King County Interlibrary Loan, and Libraries Unlimited

Our warm friends in Cholamandal Artists' Village, Banyan Teacher Centre, INTACH, and Crafts Council, India

The supportive Indian community in Seattle, including P. P. I.

Sangeet Natak Akademi, New Delhi

P. R. Thippeswamy

L. S. Rajagopalan

Mughavai Rajamanickam

Indira Seshagiri Rao

Raghavendra Rao

Krishna Kumar Marar

Chinna Oommen

K. S. Gopal and family

Joseph Kunnath

Dharampal

Ram Swarup

Premeela Gurumurthy

V. S. Sharma

Shree Coorg

Lou Corbett

Mary Orr

A. D. Edward Raj

And all the caring people at Chautauqua School, Cub Scouts, and Vashon sports who gave Manu the extra attention he needed while this book was being written!

Map of South India

GOA

VISHAKHAPATNA

HYDERABAD

BIJAPUR

AMARAVATI VIJAYAWADA

ANDHRA
PRADESH

BELGAUM

HAMPI

CHITRADURGA

KARNATAKA

(MADRAS)
CHENNAI

MANGALORE BANGALORE

CHOLAMANDAL

MYSORE VELLORE

PONDICHERRY

TAMIL NADU

(CALICUT)
KOZHIKODE COIMBATORE

KARAIKAL

THANJAVUR
(TANJORE)

KERALA

COCHIN

MADURAI

(TRIVANDRUM)
THIRUVANANTHAPURAM

KANNIYAKUMARI

Introduction

India, the world's largest democracy with one-sixth of the world's population, has thousands of stories. Many tales come from South India, where video buses speed past fine old temples and Indian satellites fly over calm fields of sugarcane. South India, where even now stories are being shared as cowbells ring, motorcycles roar, loudspeakers blare, and clothes are pounded clean with steady beats. These tales are told today, as before, to teach history and morals, to look at current events, to entertain, and to offer devotion.

Using This Book

We hope this book will help you to explore South India and her stories, whether you are a student, teacher, storyteller, librarian, parent, or armchair traveler. Of course, India is one country, there is no sharp border dividing north and south. Events in one region have often affected events in the other—from the rule of powerful dynasties to the influence of strong religious and political leaders. We have, however, stressed material on the south in this book because such information is still less widely available.

Basic facts about the region and its history, arts, and lifestyles are given first. The second chapter then presents storytelling techniques, profiles several tellers, and provides riddles, images, and ideas from South Indian storytelling to use in your own writing and telling.

The stories that follow reflect the cultures of South India, although some of the tales are enjoyed throughout India. They are grouped by

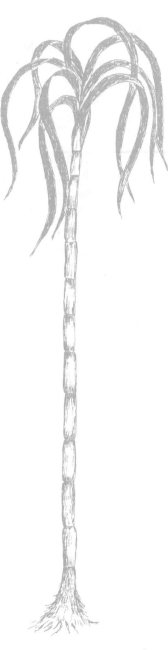

Sugarcane, a favorite snack.

themes to introduce important values found in the south today. Each chapter begins with proverbs, book excerpts, or comments from South Indian friends along with a brief introduction. When needed, short notes precede individual tales, and in the back you will find more information on story sources and folklore types, along with a glossary and index.

To help with follow-up and further research, we have included a bibliography, a resource list of bookstores and centers, development groups that appreciate help, Internet sites, and a calendar of South Indian festival days. Throughout the book are Paramasivam's illustrations, many based on *kolam* floor decorations described in Chapter 1. Color photos from our friends and our files will also help you travel visually to the land of these stories.

Setting the Stage

These stories can be read silently or aloud by various ages, and told by students, teachers, librarians, or other storytellers in home and community. We have tried to write Indian words in a way to make them both recognizable and pronounceable, but the sounds still differ from the music of the original languages. When you say the words out loud, use these basic vowel sounds and then try to find a native speaker to help you: i = **bee**, a = **father**, aa = **ahh**, o = **oh**, oo = **boot**, u = **boot**, e = **temple**, ai = **pie**.

If this book is used in a class to learn about India, you might want the students to first examine possible stereotypes about India: that all women have terrible status, that all men wear turbans, that almost everyone is poor and sleeps in the streets, that India is pretty much the same all over. Then, as you explore South India, let your setting provide information as well. Use the resource section to help you locate South Indian maps, pictures, writing, pen pals, videos, objects, and music to share. Try to find an Indian student or friend who can add to your study (if not in person, perhaps over the Internet). If you will be telling the tales, see Chapter 2 for suggestions about props, language, and story setting.

No matter how you use this book, we hope that you enjoy yourself. Story sharing, through telling or reading, is a wonderful way to travel both inside and outside yourself. As you dip into this book, remember a tale about Tenali Raman, the famous South Indian trickster, who once painted three short green lines on a palace wall. When the king asked what they were, Tenali Raman said, "A cow eating grass."

"But where is the cow?" asked the king.

Tenali Raman replied, "Please use your imagination, Sir. Then you will see that he has finished and gone on home."

With this guide, too, use your imagination. Find out more, fill in the blanks, create your own adaptation of a South Indian story. Take a tale and share it somewhere, somehow. For that is the way of the storyteller.

Chapter One

Welcome to South India

*What distinguishes the South from the North is
its robust conservatism: its genius for preserving
and using the old as the foundation for the new.*
(Spell 1987, 136)

*This is the shared dimension of experience never
lacking in South India: the beyond keeps breaking
in upon the present; it can never be ignored.*
(Shulman 1985, 5)

Vanakkam. Welcome to South India, a place where jasmine flowers grace the hair and coconuts grace the land. Although a region of many riches, it is not yet well known to most Americans. Mention India and people think of the Taj Mahal, the Himalayan mountains, the Ganges river, crowded Calcutta. All of these images are Indian, but they are from North India. A journey to the south reveals new treasures as the past shapes the present, and science centers, bullock carts, nuclear energy plants, and towering temples are all equally at home.

*Mango is a popular summer
fruit in South India.*

The Land

India on the map points south, with the four southern states at the bottom nearing the equator. Like a huge tabletop, the Deccan plateau covers much of the southern peninsula, from the tall hills of the Western Ghats near the west coast to the milder Eastern Ghats on the opposite side. Near the coasts are fertile plains and endless beaches. Rivers—the Kaveri, Godavari, Krishna—run through the region, creating fine agricultural lands. With generous sunshine and two monsoons spreading rains, the south boasts of varied vegetation. Southern forests nurture spices, teak, cashew, bamboo, and soft wood, while the plains and coasts give abundant rice, coconuts, sugarcane, and other food crops. In the western hills, with one of the highest rainfalls in India, tea, coffee, and rubber grow well.

Mountain ranges across the top of the region have often protected the south from invasions by northern forces. While humans had relative peace to develop a rich culture, animals also roamed freely. Today in southern forests and wildlife sanctuaries are elephants, gaurs (wild oxen), leopards, monkeys, tigers, snakes, deer, wild dogs, peacocks and other birds.

Cultural Characteristics, Roots, and Values

India, although it has a unity nourished by certain common values, stories, and heritage, it is also rich in diversity. The south, although part of a larger whole, still has a different flavor. Large and small things set it apart from the north: a taste for coffee and rice; a religious conservatism with a strong sense of devotion; a heritage of tolerance; a passion for flowers; a warmer year-round climate; the blessings of coconuts and sandalwood; the beauty of its bronzes and silks; and its traditions of music and dance.

The foundation for today's south came from the Dravidian people whose culture seemed in place by about the third or second millennium B.C.E. Although opinions are mixed about the origin of these people, the four major languages spoken today in the south and the worldviews still held there spring from a base formed by these Dravidians.

Dravidian culture worshipped nature's powers and respected women's powers as well. Susan Wadley, in *The Powers of Tamil Women,* concludes after a review of marriage, puberty, birth customs, and health care, that "In general, women in the south live longer, are more valued, and are more critical to the natal (birth) kin than are North Indian women" (Wadley 1980, 161). The matriarchal family, with inheritance passed through the female, seems to have been important early on in Dravidian life. The Mother-goddess was often worshipped, as were village deities. These village guardians were frequently female, but might have a non-human form—a rock or tree that would protect the village in exchange for offerings and prayer. Snake worship was also important to Dravidians, as well as the worship of heroes who died in battle, spirits, animals like the tiger or bull, and sacred trees. Agricultural objects were frequently honored, too, in South India (Hanur 1991).

Aryan influence from North India mixed with this base of Dravidian thought as some Aryan people settled in the south from about 800 B.C.E. The resulting worldview is reflected in values still held today: a belief in the sacred; a respect for elders, parents, and learning; a regard for friendship, patience, generosity, hospitality; and an admiration for heroes and for purity.

Snakes are important symbols in South Indian myth and art.

A Brief History

Early Years

The Stone Age, however, occurred before the rise of the Dravidian culture. Although it is difficult to know how long humans have lived in the south, noted Indian historian Nilakanta Sastri suggests that "the antiquity of human life in these regions goes back about 300,000 years, but for quite a long time man lived at what is known as the Old Stone (Paleolithic) Age" (Sastri 1987, 49). Humans passed through several stages as they turned to farming and a more settled life. Remains from the Megalithic culture in the south, which started perhaps by 1100 B.C.E., include various tombs, iron tools, ornaments, and pottery. Such pots, black inside and red outside, often had marks for good fortune, deciphered by Clyde Ahmed Winters (Winters 1992, 455).

Marks meaning: virtue, to increase, greatness, to tie, abundance.

As the south developed, it reached beyond its borders. Culture and commerce grew together and South Indians took to the seas to trade their rich resources. Indian spices were a must for making baked lamb, a favorite dish in Rome 2,000 years ago. Shiploads of spices (cardamom, cinnamon, cloves, turmeric), muslin, silks, ivory, tortoise shells, and precious stones were carried off to Rome. In return, Rome sent lead, glassware, copper, liquor, coins, and traders who settled in South Indian ports.

The Arabs also came to trade, then stayed. They favored the coastal area of the southwest with its excellent ports, as did the Jewish traders and others who started coming in the first century C.E. (Cochin, Kerala, still has a beautiful Jewish synagogue). Those who dealt with the rulers found them to be honest and efficient, as Benjamin of Tudela wrote in 1179 C.E.: "The nation is very trustworthy. Whenever foreign merchants enter their port, three secretaries repair on their vessels to write down their names. The king thereupon grants them security for their property, which they may even leave in the open fields without any guard" (Ayyar 1966, 65).

Great Kingdoms, Great Learning

As trade grew, kingdoms did too. One early northern dynasty, the Mauryas, which produced the great emperor Ashok, extended its borders into the south. But most of the northern kingdoms, even the illustrious dynasties of the Kushans and the Guptas, had very limited influence in the south. One important early southern dynasty was that of the Cholas. Great seafarers and temple builders, by 1025 C.E. they controlled much of South India and Sri Lanka, with bases as well in Burma, Malaysia, and Indonesia. In 1077, a Chola mission to China offered "pearls as big as peas, camphor, the teeth of rhino, textiles, incense and perfumes, medicinal plants, borax, spices, and essence of roses" (Nayak and Gopal 1990, 377).

The rule of the Cholas, and various other South Indian rulers, was often marked by justice and a concern for the welfare of subjects. Peaceful protest against unfair practices was possible and rule by the *panchayat* (local governing bodies of elders) was common. Many temples were built with great skill. One in Thanjavur city has the tallest temple tower in India, 64-meters high, with a top piece carved from a granite block weighing almost 80 metric tons and pulled into place up a ramp nearly 6-kilometers long.

Indian knowledge shone not only in temple architecture but in many fields during these times, from north to south. The use of zero and place value originated in India, and the study of astronomy was well advanced. Medical sciences had identified a wide range of natural healing plants; various vaccination and surgical techniques were skilled and effective. Small gold and cooper coins were used in the south, with pictures of kings, elephants, horses, or the sun stamped upon them. Iron made in South India was of a superior quality. In farming, irrigation techniques included the use of numerous huge irrigation tanks.

Yet even as the arts and sciences developed in the south, battles raged both against northern invaders and amongst the southern kingdoms and faiths. Armies thundered across the plains with cavalry, infantry, chariots, and fighting elephants, but rarely did one power manage to control much of the south.

During the fourteenth century, northern Muslim kingdoms pushed south but, in 1347, Muslim officers in the Deccan rebelled against Delhi and formed the Bahmani kingdom. It remained a center of Islamic culture in the south until the sixteenth century and then it broke into five separate Muslim kingdoms. Rulers of one such kingdom, Bijapur, created an architectural wonder: Gol Gumbaz, a tomb with the second largest round dome in the world—43.9 meters in diameter, without any pillars. In Golconda, another of these Muslim kingdoms, the Golconda fort was an engineering marvel with more than 11 kilometers of outer walls built from huge granite blocks. It had eight gates, pipes for hot and cold water, and an ingenious acoustic warning design—even a hand clap at the entrance could be heard a long distance away near the summit.

The last of the great southern dynasties, the Vijayanagar Empire, was formed in 1336, in part to balance this growing Muslim influence. Vijayanagar was an empire with far-flung trading interests in Southeast Asia, China, Arabia, and Portugal. Its greatest ruler, Krishnadeva Raya, was a writer, a patron of the arts, and a disciplined warrior who arose before dawn, exercised with clay weights and a sword, then wrestled and rode on horseback, all before his morning bath (Sastri 1987). Vijayanagar's powerful army included 1,000 elephants, each one with sharp knives on its tusks and eight soldiers fighting from its back. The empire was also one of beauty as Abdul Razaq, a Muslim envoy, described in 1443:

> Vijayanagar is such that the pupil of the eye has never seen a place like it and the ear of intelligence has never been informed that there existed anything to equal it in the world. . . . In the long bazaars, flowers are sold everywhere. The people could not live without flowers. . . . In this agreeable locality, as well as in the king's palace, one sees numerous streams and channels formed of polished, chiseled stone (Dubey and Grewal 1990, 205).

However, this grand empire also fell when the separate Muslim forces to its north formed a coalition and destroyed the capital city in 1565. About this time, in the sixteenth and seventeenth centuries, the powerful rule of the Mughals dominated the north and extended into the south. Although their spirit lives still in the splendid buildings and art they developed, their rule peaked under the wise emperor Akbar and then began to decay. The lack of a dominant ruling power in India after Aurangzeb, the last strong Mughal ruler, played into the hands of foreign powers seeking India's silk, spices, and gold.

Elephants were used in wars, at royal courts, and in temples.

British Rule

In 1498, Vasco de Gama landed in Kerala and more Portuguese soon followed, aggressively seeking converts and commerce. The British, as the East India Company, arrived later and in 1639 purchased land in Chennai (Madras) which became Fort St. George, an important center of British rule. The Dutch, French, and Danes came as well and struggles intensified for control of India and its resources. The British eventually triumphed and by 1818 ruled most of South (and North) India. In 1858, following a strong Indian resistance movement, the British government took control from the East India Company.

Under British rule, many traditional industries and crafts were ruined, the economy greatly weakened, the educational system berated, and Indian culture belittled. Although some Europeans marveled at the wisdom found in India over the centuries, many remained aloof from Indians and wrapped themselves in their comfortable and familiar cultures. A speech by a prominent British official, Lord MacCauley, in 1835, reflects this colonial viewpoint:

> I have never found one scholar (of oriental studies) who could deny that a single shelf of a good European library was worth the whole native literature of India and Arabia. . . . When we pass from works of imagination to works in which facts are recorded and general principles investigated, the superiority of the Europeans becomes absolutely immeasurable. It is, I believe, no exaggeration to say that all the historical information which has been collected from all the books written in the Sanskrit (Indian) language is less valuable than what may be found in the most paltry abridgment used at preparatory schools in England (Dharampal 1971, LXI).

Under British rule, an extensive network of transportation and communication was developed. The British created English-based cultural and educational institutions. The Indian population used these systems to gain ideas and information from outside India and to communicate across regional linguistic differences as they worked to regain their land and sovereignty.

Independence

Resistance grew to the British over the years, in the north and south. In South India, freedom fighters included Velu Thambi, Kattabomman, Tippu Sultan, and others who fought in bloody battles; V. O. Chidambaram Pillai who started an Indian shipping company; the poet Bharathi and those who used weapons of words and art; along with the many who followed Gandhi, protesting with nonviolent means.

In 1947, after riots, fasts, and protests, freedom finally came to all of India. A government by Indians for Indians was formed, much like the British model: a democratic, elected leadership with a Parliament of two Houses, a Prime Minister, and a President. A government that pledged to promote economic and educational growth, to institute needed land reforms, to outlaw untouchability. As the world's largest democracy planned its future, four separate southern states were created in the 1950s, with borders based largely on linguistic areas. In addition, the Union Territory, consisting of former French enclaves, was created with the southern city of Pondicherry as its capital.

South India Today

Although the south boasts rich resources of human energy, culture, and nature, there are also problems. When the monsoons bring too much rain, floods damage people and crops. When the rains fail, drought can result, with problems of lack of food, water, and hydroelectric power supply. Corruption in government, business, and everyday life has become a major problem. The environment, including forestland, heritage sites, and wildlife, is threatened by rapid development and the demands of a very large population. More effort is needed to improve education and health as well as the position of women and of the lower castes. Recently, too, a growing Westernization of values and lifestyles has been felt, especially in urban areas.

Yet South India is working hard, along with the Indian Central Government, to make needed changes. Accomplishments have been made in areas of technology, industry, science, and education. India now has both rockets and nuclear power, while consumer goods of all types are available for those who can afford them. Laws have been passed to protect those with less power, and changes have been made in the economy to help encourage more growth. And a feeling of pride, strengthened by the fiftieth anniversary of Independence, helps to temper the influence of Western media and consumer products.

Women in South India, too, are working for change through various womens' groups and womens' publications. The exciting true stories of female leaders include, to mention only two of many: Mrs. Beevi, from Kerala, who was the first woman judge of the Supreme Court in 1989 and, in 1997, the first woman governor of Tamil Nadu; and South Indian Nibha Namboodiri, who recently became one of only two female elephant *mahouts* (trainers) in India.

Many people are also helping those in need and protecting heritage and the environment in projects like these (also see Appendix).

Project Tiger, launched to protect Indian tigers, raised the tiger population in Bandipur National Park, Karnataka, from 11 in 1972 to 74 in 1995.

DakshinaChitra in Tamil Nadu runs a new, unique open-air museum of South Indian houses and crafts, building pride in South Indian heritage.

INTACH supports projects to restore historic sites, preserve culture, and teach children about conservation.

Integrated Rural Technology Centre, Kerala, promotes efficient wood cooking stoves, solar water heating, small windmills, and wise use of village resources.

South Indian States, an Overview

Tamil Nadu

Capital: Chennai (Madras). Major cities: Coimbatore, Madurai
Area: 130,058 sq. km
Population: 56 million (1991 census)
Language: Tamil
Major rivers: Kaveri, Vaigai
Major crops: sugarcane, millet, rice, maize, cotton

Vanakkam—*greeting in Tamil.*

At its southern tip, in Kanniyakumari, one can see both sunrise and sunset; in the cool Nilgiri hills, even the summer sun is bearable. In its rice fields, abundant rice grows, and along its coast stretch splendid beaches with villages of hardy fishers. Tamil Nadu, land of the Tamil people, is a place of beauty and tradition. Besides the Tamils, small numbers of indigenous people also call this area home, including the Todas who dwell in the Nilgiri hills.

An unusual part of Tamil heritage is the Tamil Sangam. There were said to be three of these gatherings of poets and writers thousands of years ago. The most famous is the last Sangam with almost 500 poet-members who assembled regularly in Madurai city in the first centuries C.E., producing more than 2,000 poems. Tamil Nadu was also the home of the Pallava, Pandya, and Chola kingdoms. During their reigns came, at various times, overseas trade, lofty temples and thriving temple towns, the births of important saints, beautifully sculpted bronze statues and stone carvings, as well as dance and music traditions still shared today.

In modern times, the Tamil film industry has flourished. Huge billboards of movie stars tower above busy streets and movie theaters are often crowded. Two recent chief ministers of Tamil Nadu, M. G. Ramachandran and Jayalalitha, were first Tamil movie stars. South of Chennai, crocodiles are the stars in one of South India's most interesting banks, the Crocodile Bank. In this lovely open-air sanctuary and research center, visitors wander the grounds viewing hundreds of crocodiles in varied settings.

Andhra Pradesh

Capital: Hyderabad. Major cities: Vishakhapatnam, Vijayawada

Area: 275,045 sq. km

Population: 66.5 million

Language: Telugu spoken by the majority, with Urdu also used
around Hyderabad

Major rivers: Krishna, Godavari

Major crops: rice, sugarcane, tobacco, millet, oilseeds

Namaskaaramu—*greeting in Telugu.*

Andhra's long coastline of about 960 kilometers hosts India's only submarine base, and Andhra's rich plains produce much rice. At the former Buddhist centers of Amaravati and Nagarjunakonda, treasures from the past are on display yet in busy Hyderabad, the software industry thrives. Many Muslims live in Hyderabad, while the nomadic Banjara people, famous for their colorful embroidery, move from place to place across the state.

Early in this region, the Satavahanas ruled, to be followed by other rulers and kingdoms including the Muslim Bahmani kingdom. The princely state of Hyderabad, created in 1724 by a nobleman, Nizam-ul-Mulk, was ruled by a line of Muslim Nizams, under British influence, until Independence. During that time it had its own railways, post, currency, parks, and much wealth: Nizam Osman Ali Pasha, who ruled in the twentieth century, had rooms full of gold, acres of land, a 162-carat diamond, 10 huge emeralds, and enough pearls to cover the roof of his palace (Allen and Dwivedi 1984, 268).

For many years, before and after Independence, the people of Andhra wished to have their own separate state, but meetings and committees on the issue didn't produce results. So on October 19, 1952, patriot Sri Potti Sreeramulu used a traditional weapon: he started a hunger strike. Although many leaders, including Prime Minister Nehru himself, pleaded with him to stop, he would not. After 58 days without eating, on December 15, 1952, he died for the dream of statehood. Chaos followed and weeks later, Andhra Pradesh came into being as the first state in India formed on a linguistic basis.

Karnataka

Capital: Bangalore. Major cities: Mysore, Belgaum, Mangalore

Area: 192,204 sq. km

Population: over 45 million.

Language: Kannada spoken by over 70 percent of the population, Tulu and Konkani spoken along the coast, with Kodava spoken in Kodagu (Coorg)

Major rivers: Kaveri, Krishna.

Major crops: rice, ragi, wheat, sugarcane, timber

Namaskaara—*greeting in Kannada.*

Karnataka has a coast about 330-kilometers long, the highest waterfall in India (250-meter-high Jog Falls), and plentiful land on the Deccan plateau, including the haunting ruins of the old Vijayanagar kingdom. In the beautiful hilly area of Kodagu are the Kodava people who speak their own Dravidian language. On the southern coast, a rich tradition of ballads is found among those who speak Tulu, another Dravidian language.

From its early days, Karnataka has been home to many Jains, who have contributed to its literature and the arts. A famous landmark in the state, and one of the tallest monolithic statues in the world, is a 17.4-meter statue of the Jaina saint Gomatesvara, carved out of a single granite boulder. Standing in an ageless silence, the statue can be seen up to 26 kilometers away today as it has for a thousand years. Besides the Jains, both Muslim and Hindu rulers from north and south have thrived in this state, including the maharajas of Mysore whose palaces still rest proudly in Mysore city.

Karnataka today, with its strong industrial base, is known for sandalwood, silk, and software. The state's large network of research and development organizations—more than 50 technical engineering colleges and 60 polytechnic colleges—produce about 20,000 technically skilled professionals yearly, making Karnataka a leader in high technology today.

Kerala

Capital: Thiruvananthapuram (Trivandrum). Major cities: Cochin, Kozhikode (Calicut)

Area: 38,800 sq. km

Population: 30 million

Language: Malayalam

Major river: Periyar

Major crops: rice, tapioca, spices, coir, cashews, rubber, coconuts

വന്ദനം.

Vandanam—*greeting in Malayalam.*

Kerala's destiny is linked to water, with a coastline of 580 kilometers, over 40 rivers, and more than 1,000 canals. A high annual rainfall helps coconuts thrive, keeps the land green, and nourishes the unique rain forest of Silent Valley. Kerala is a land of tolerance among religions: Muslims of Arab descent mix with Hindus and the Christians who make up one-third of the population. Communities also exist in Kerala that follow the matriarchal system of lineage where property is handed down through the female line.

Under the rule of the Chera kings long ago and later rulers of small kingdoms, Kerala's natural resources were nourished. A sense of beauty, a regard for neatness, and an industrious spirit have been remarked upon for years here, as Major General Walker wrote in 1820:

> (One sees) a neatness of dress, and a cleanliness of person from head to heel. The same neatness may be seen through every part of the countryside. It is displayed in their agriculture. It is not fine houses, but nature and the broad canopy of heaven that they contemplate with delight. They have everywhere under their eye magnificent and fertile landscapes. These they improve and ornament by planting fruit trees which refresh the traveller (Dharampal 1971, 209).

In 1956, Kerala state was formed and soon became the first state in the world to elect a Communist government. Kerala is also home to such groups as Kerala Sastra Sahitya Parishat that promote science study through science marches and other projects. The people in Kerala are proud of two recent records: Kerala has both India's highest literacy rate (almost 100 percent) and its lowest maternal mortality rate—only 87 deaths per 100,000 live births while the all-India figure is about 450 (National Council of Applied Economic Research, in Narasimhan 1997).

Religious Roots

In a region as large and diverse as South India, there are many ways of thinking. Although some South Indians do not believe in any god or religion, most South Indians still do.

The Various Religions

Two of the earliest religions in South India were Buddhism and Jainism. Buddhists and Jains believe strongly in nonviolence, are against *caste* inequalities, and encourage respect for monks and the founders of their faiths. In earlier times, both religions influenced South Indian rulers and Jaina writers contributed a great deal to South Indian literature, especially in Karnataka. However, the Buddhist following dwindled in the early centuries C.E., while the Jains were weakened as the Hindu *Bhakti* devotional movement grew from the fifth century.

Islam came first to South India through trade with Arabs and has been followed ever since in various areas of the south. It is built on the belief in Allah and his creations, as revealed in the holy scriptures, including the *Qur'an*, and through a line of prophets ending with Muhammad. Religious practices include the "Five Pillars of Islam": a declaration of faith and belief, daily worship five times a day, helping the poor, fasting during the month of Ramadan, and making a pilgrimage to holy Makkah.

Christianity entered India in various ways: through St. Thomas who was said to have arrived in 52 C.E., St. Frances Xavier and others in the sixteenth century, and then through Protestant missionaries who helped to spread educational and social services. With the varied denominations seeking converts across the south, discussions and arguments sometimes took place:

> Once a Dutch Reformed Minister tried to win over a Catholic converted by St. Frances Xavier. After listening to the minister, a Tamil Catholic replied, "Since St. Frances has done many miracles and raised five people or more from the dead, if you wish to convert us, please begin by bringing back to life at least a dozen dead people . . . cure all our sick people, make our sea richer in fish than it is at present, and when you have done this, it will be time to consider what reply to make to you" (Bayly 1989, 330).

Paths of Hinduism

Although these varied faiths exist in the south, Hinduism remains the predominant religion. It is a religion embracing many ideas and beliefs, many ways to find *moksha*, spiritual release from birth and rebirth. One of the most popular paths is through *bhakti*, or personal devotion and love. Bhakti gained great popularity by the seventh century in South India, then spread throughout India, and is strong yet today. Saints from backgrounds rich and poor, including several women, started this movement when they used great devotion and love, instead of too many rituals and sacrifices, to reach their god. Two groups of devotees were important and their stories are popular even today. The Alvars were 12 devotees who worshipped Lord Vishnu, while the Nayanmars were 63 devotees who worshipped Lord Siva through songs such as this:

"Like flawless music of the lute, like the evening moon,

like the blowing southern breeze, like the young expansive spring,

like the lotus pond humming with bees,

is the shade of the feet of the Lord, my Master."

Appar, a Nayanmar saint (Raghavan 1979, 86)

Besides the way of bhakti, there are paths to moksha using yoga and meditation, good works done selflessly, knowledge and reasoning. An Ultimate Being, called *Brahman*, is found in Hinduism—difficult to contemplate and compared to an infinite ocean, with the Hindu gods as Its waves. These more accessible gods offer believers help in daily life and for other lifetimes: *Siva, Vishnu, Kali, Ganesha*, and others (see Chapter 4 and Glossary) are often worshipped in small village temples as well as in the majestic temples of the south.

Ganesha with snake belt, sweets, a lotus, a noose, and goad, with a mouse always near.

For many centuries, in many cities, this type of grand temple was very important. It provided educational opportunities; helped with medical care at times; dispensed justice; and employed various craftspeople, artists, laborers, and scholars. From earliest morning until late at night, it stood open to most of the community, providing for spiritual needs while its festivals gave entertainment to all, helping briefly to integrate various levels of society.

Daily worship at home has also been usual over the years, with offerings of flowers, coconut and fruits, incense, camphor, chants, or prayers. Pilgrimages to holy places, keeping of rituals and fasts, and support of the holy and needy are also valued by most Hindus today.

Reforms in Hinduism

Although many people over the years worshipped with true faith and pure hearts, problems and prejudices crept into the practice of Hinduism. One source of trouble was the *caste* system that began to dictate the work and duties of all in society, putting people into roles passed on for generations. From priests and kings to weavers and butchers, all had their place in the caste system and they stayed in that place. Over the years, the system became too strict, with unfair differences including ideas of who was pure (the high castes) and who was polluted (the lowest castes and *Harijans*). Over the years, many southern saints and sages fought against the caste system, as well as against the meaningless practices and rituals performed at times:

> "There are only no castes but two if you want me to tell,
>
> One, the good men who help the poor in distress,
>
> The other, that will not so help."
>
> > Avvaiyar, Tamil sage who attacked social ills
> > through poetry, first century C.E.
> > (Rajagopalachari 1971, 9)

> "When they see a serpent carved in stone, they pour milk on it
>
> > (to worship),
>
> if a real serpent comes, they say, 'Kill, kill.'
>
> To the servant of God, who could eat if served, they say, 'Go, go.'
>
> But to the stone statue which cannot eat, they offer dishes of food."
>
> > Basavanna, saint in Karnataka
> > who promoted equality, twelfth century
> > (Raghavan 1979, 106)

"Why dost thou again and again abuse a pariah (Harijan)?

Are not his blood and flesh and thine one?

The (same) deity animates the entire world."

Vemana, a sage whose sayings are known
in Andhra Pradesh, seventeenth century
(Brown 1986, 215)

The Arts of South India

Stories are not only told in South India, but are shared through and influenced by a rich weave of music, art, drama, and movement. Several related arts are briefly profiled below to show this integration, but for material on the large, ever-growing field of South Indian literature, please see the Resources section.

Dance

With the tilt of a head, a wave of an arm, the sound of ankle bells beating joyfully, the South Indian dancer offers devotion and shares tales of the gods. Dancing thrived hundreds of years ago in the south as a temple art, especially during the ninth and tenth centuries, but suffered a decline under the British. Fortunately in this century, dedicated artists worked to bring back several forms of dance.

One of the greatest South Indian dancers of the twentieth century was Balasaraswati, who helped to revive the famed *Bharata Natyam* dance known best in Tamil Nadu. She followed a very strenuous regime of practice and study, teaching many the true meaning of the dance through her acts and her words: "The dancer who dissolves her identity in rhythm and music makes her body an instrument, at least for the duration of the dance, for the experience and expression of spirit" (Dubey and Grewal 1990, 82).

Bharata Natyam and the more lyrical, softer *Mohini Attam* from Kerala are important solo dance forms, vibrant and expressive. *Kuchipudi* (from Andhra) can be presented as a solo dance and also as a dance drama to share scenes from famous Hindu stories.

In *Teyyam*, a ritual dance form in parts of the west coast, a human dancer moves into a trancelike state in which he acts as a god, spirit, or local hero. The headcrowns and palm leaf costumes, make-up, drumming, rituals and songs, combined with the dancer's belief and the crowd's fervor create an unforgettable experience as characters of myth and legend seem to come alive.

Not to be forgotten are the folk dances still shared especially in villages during festivals and holidays. One favorite is the popular *kolattam* stick dance, where each dancer holds two sticks and uses them to beat out lovely rhythms with the sticks of other dancers while all move to create circles, squares, and other designs on the floor. In a related folk dance, similar patterns are clapped by hands alone.

Theater Arts

Kathakali dance-drama in Kerala is becoming world famous as a powerful feast for the eyes, ears, and spirit. While drums sound and singers chant, colorfully made-up and costumed actors portray Hindu myths and epics through mime and dance alone. *Yakshagana*, in neighboring Karnataka, is a dance-drama form in which speech, dance, and music share many plays written from the sixteenth century on. Tamil Nadu has *Terukuttu*, a popular street theater with plenty of humor and color. All of these forms are usually performed outside, for long hours, to large crowds.

Modern drama in South India is an active field. Western plays are acted in the southern cities along with new dramas, written and directed by talented South Indians, which often weave Indian roots into powerful contemporary expressions. Several modern film directors, especially from Kerala, are also well respected for their sensitive films exploring modern South Indian life.

Less common now, but still enjoyed, are the puppet traditions of South India. They range from the large leather shadow puppets of Andhra Pradesh that can tower up to six feet, to the wooden marionettes in Karnataka, patterned after the Yakshagana drama, and the elaborate Kathakali hand puppets of Kerala, an art form that had almost died out recently until a young artist, G. Venu, worked hard to revive it.

Music

Karnatic music, the classical music of the south, is based on concepts of *raga* (a melodic sequence of notes often reflecting certain times and moods), *tala* (rhythmic beat, cyclic in nature), and *bhava* (emotions), with improvisation often used and much enjoyed. Purandaradasa, born in Karnataka, is known as the father of Karnatic music. After him came three great composers—Tyagaraja, Muthuswamy Dikshitar, and Syama Sastry—whose songs are still enjoyed in different ways: "The sweetness of Tyagaraja's music can be enjoyed straightaway like grapes, that of Sastry's like the banana which needs a quick peeling, while to relish Dikshitar's music you must use the effort of cracking a hard coconut to get the sweetness of the fruit inside" (Khandpur 1994, 43).

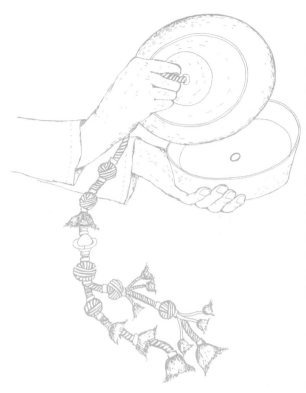

Traditional instruments used in both Karnatic and folk music are rich and varied. They include stringed instruments from the simple *tambura* (which gives a drone sound) to the sophisticated *veena*; bamboo flutes; various bells; drums of different sizes, shapes, and materials. Film music, from North and South Indian movies, is also very popular in South India. From sunrise to past sunset, it spills out of radios, loudspeakers, and buses. Devotional songs and chants sung in worship, as well as folk songs for work and leisure, are also shared.

Martial Arts and Yoga

Yoga is known in the West largely as a physical practice. It means more in India, and is followed by some in the south as a strict discipline and meditation to find spiritual release. Students

Kamsale instrument used in ballad singing.

from around the world come to study with several yoga masters in South India, while the physical postures and breathing practices are taught in various Indian schools.

Although there are several kinds of martial arts in the south, the most well known is the *kalaripayattu* of Kerala, which has also inspired several South Indian performing art forms. Taking its name from *kalari*, the military gymnasium where it was taught, the art combines massage to make the body supple and exercises, with and without weapons of wood and metal. Kalaripayattu is taught in several places still, and today's training resembles that observed by the Portuguese Duarte Barbosa in the sixteenth century:

> When they are seven, they are taught many tricks of nimbleness and dexterity, to dance and turn about and to twist on the ground, to take royal leaps . . . and they become so loose jointed and supple that they make their bodies turn as if they had no bones. Next they teach them to use the weapon to which they are most inclined, some with bows and arrows, some with poles, but most with swords, and are ever practicing (Ayyar 1966, 131).

Visual Arts and Crafts

South Indian arts have been a feast to the eyes and to the spirit for years, astonishing some British observers, like Dr. Helenus Scott who wrote in 1790:

> We have kept our eyes in this country on diamonds and pepper
> and pearls while we have neglected the substances that would have
> improved our manufactures or created new arts among us. . . .
> These arts improved by the practice of so many years might afford
> a matter of entertainment and instruction to the most enlightened
> philosopher of Europe. . . . It is a field in which there are so many
> beautiful objects that one is distracted with the variety (Dharampal
> 1971, 268).

Today from homes, street stalls, and shops still come gold or silver chains and ornaments, palm mats, wooden toys of village life, handmade paper, baskets of many sizes and materials, and elaborate carvings for homes and temples. Hand loom weavers (often working on pit looms sunk into the floor) and other textile workers produce a range of cloth including exquisite silks and lovely tie-dyed or hand printed cottons.

South Indian art is often devotional in spirit, or tied to festivals: elegant bronze statues of Siva; giant, bright terra-cotta figures of village deities; large wooden statues of *bhuta* spirits; stone carvings of gods large and small; glowing brass lamps or simple clay oil lamps; clever festival toys including pinwheels, small drums, little carts, palm puppets, and more.

Graceful, temporary carpets, to greet guests and gods daily, cover the floor or ground for festivals, rituals, and special days. These beautiful decorations are made outdoors using powdered white stone with colors added for special days, and inside with rice paste meant to be eaten by insects, birds, and little animals. Such a design, called *kolam*, *rangoli,* or *muggu*, is created in various ways: sometimes upon a grid of dots, sometimes bounded by a circle, sometimes with a freer hand. Geometric patterns, flowers, butterflies, snakes, and many more designs are used. The world's largest kolam was made by Indians in Malaysia in the fall of 1997 when 450 volunteers took 18 hours to make the huge 70 x 40.5 meter design!

A number of exciting modern artists are found across South India. For a contemporary look at South Indian sculptors, *see Contemporary Indian Sculpture: The Madras Metaphor* by Josef James, 1993. Although many artists in the four states work on their own, one unusual cooperative artists' village, Cholamandal, is found south of Chennai. Started in 1966, it is now a place of beauty near the sea, with studios, homes, a gallery, and quiet places to share stories and art.

Daily Life in South India

In the folktale section of this book, South India comes alive in stories, the very stories children in South India might still hear. Some of the stories will be familiar and some may be new, but many will, in some way, share a little of the region. The more you can picture the life behind the stories, the richer the tales become. You can't fly by jet to South India this moment, but by using the lists below, you can fly in your imagination.

Across South India, however, are many varying lifestyles: of village, town, or city; from rich to poor; of the hills, plains, and coast. Since it is impossible to share cultural details about each lifestyle, a range of details is provided so that you can think of the different ways you might live, if you were born in South India.

Your home might:

    ⊰ be near a forest, a hill, a river, a tea estate, rice fields, a large plain, a small village, in a large town, or a giant city;

    ⊰ be on the sidewalk, or made of concrete, mud and thatch, brick, perhaps with a courtyard or a porch;

    ⊰ have some plants nearby: trees with coconut, mango, jackfruit, or tamarind; a large banyan or a big banana plant; maybe spices, tea and coffee, vegetables, and flowers—lotus, marigolds, jasmine, roses, and more;

    ⊰ have animals near it: stray dogs but very few cats (for pets are not so common), chickens, goats, water buffaloes, donkeys, cows, bullocks, pigs, birds.

At home, you might:

    ⊰ live with or near many family members, including your grandparents, aunts, and uncles, especially in smaller towns and villages;

    ⊰ pray daily to images of gods kept on a shelf, in a corner, or in a *puja* (worship) room;

    ⊰ wash clothes at the river or well, or give to a *dhobi* (laundryperson), since washing machines are not common, and have clothes ironed when the man with the mobile ironing cart comes near your home;

    ⊰ get your water from an inside or outside faucet or pump, a river, a village well;

    ⊰ walk barefoot inside and sit on floor mats, on "built-in" narrow front porches, or on chairs;

- sleep on the floor on a mat that you roll up and store by day, or on a cot;
- grind spices on a large, flat stone with a heavy stone rolling pin, and cook on wood stoves, kerosene burners, or with propane gas fed into a two burner stovetop;
- use a low toilet built into the floor, rather than a "Western style" one.

Firewood stove with bumps to support pots, tiny lamp for lighting stove, vegetable chopper with birdlike metal blade, tube for blowing flames, and spices in little cups near coconut ladle.

To eat, you might:
- be a vegetarian, although many South Indians eat some meat (but usually not daily);
- use your right hand (very neatly too!) and eat off of a metal plate or a large, clean (and biodegradable) banana leaf;
- like pickles and *chutneys* from mango, lime, mint, coconut, coriander, and more;
- eat bread which is becoming more popular, but not packaged cereal, which is hard to find and expensive;

◄ enjoy *idly* (steamed rice and grain buns), *dosa* (crisp rice pancake), flavored rices like tamarind or lemon rice, *sambar* (bean and vegetable mix), *rasam* (thin peppery broth from beans), *biryani* (spiced rice and meat), sweet *payasam* pudding;

◄ drink milky coffee or tea if you're old enough, buy bottled sodas;

◄ like to snack on: *poli* (filled sweet pancake), crispy fried *murukku*, tapioca and banana chips, and fruits—mangoes, bananas in various sizes, guavas, papayas, jackfruit, sweet sugarcane pieces, and more;

◄ chew *paan* as an adult—betel nut and lime, sometimes with various spices and sweet syrups, rolled in a fresh betel leaf.

For education, you might:

◄ go to a government school, a private English Medium (language) school, to a nonformal education classroom at night if you work, or try to learn something "on the job";

◄ use fewer materials and not as many books (they're costly), have smaller school libraries (if at all), and often do schoolwork with chalk on a slate when young;

◄ study hard, learn several languages at school, and memorize many things for big exams;

◄ wear a school uniform, along with sandals, stiff black shoes, or cool bare feet.

In your spare time, you might:

◄ sing popular film songs and listen to them on the radio or over a loudspeaker;

◄ go to movies since South India produces hundreds of films yearly, watch TV or video (with Indian and Western programs) either at your home, a neighbor's, or on a village TV set;

◄ play snakes and ladders, with kites or cars, with pebbles or shells, with dolls of wood or clay, and, rarely, with expensive dolls like Barbie and G.I. Joe now found in some city stores;

◄ enjoy playing or watching sports like cricket, soccer, or the traditional *kabbadi* tag game;

◄ play with your friends, go to a park, zoo, museum (especially in cities), or to fairs, festivals.

When you shop, you might:

- ⊰ use *rupee* coins or notes of different colors for different denominations with small change given in *paisa* (100 paisa equals one rupee);

- ⊰ go to city shops with fancy foreign and Indian goods, or open-air markets in cities, towns, and villages with piles of grains, spices, fruits, tools, and more to tempt you, or buy from a vegetable or fruit seller who comes, with a cart or basket, near your home;

- ⊰ buy *sari* cloth for women, *lungi* or *dhoti* cloth for men, ready-made clothes, or buy material for a tailor to stitch into skirts and blouses or *salwar kameez* outfits for females, and shorts, pants, shirts for males;

- ⊰ as a female—buy pretty, colorful glass bangles to wear, flowers or flower chains for your hair and the temple, along with red kumkum powder and items for worship.

For health and safety, you might:

- ⊰ have a weekly oil bath, then rub turmeric or sandalwood on your skin;

- ⊰ brush your teeth with the healthy twig of the neem tree or use a toothbrush and toothpaste;

- ⊰ try home remedies and preventions: cumin water in Kerala for health, turmeric as antiseptic and to cure eye troubles; charms and symbols to protect against evil influences;

- ⊰ use different medicines: sometimes Western, sometimes from traditional indigenous systems;

- ⊰ find out the most auspicious times to do things like travel, start a business, marry.

To marry, you might:

- ⊰ have your marriage arranged (since dating is rare) through a matrimonial ad in the newspaper, or by a relative, then have your horoscope exchanged and checked for compatibility with your prospective mate;

- ⊰ marry a relative in your extended family and community network, which is more often done in South India;

- ⊰ have a long, involved ceremony, with many rituals, much decoration in setting, dress, hand designs, along with fine feasting;

- ⊰ as a bride, wear a *thali*—a special necklace—instead of a ring and probably give a dowry.

To get around or stay in touch, you might:

- walk frequently, perhaps have a bike, ride in a cycle or auto rickshaw, bus or train, but have a car only if you were very wealthy;

- have a computer, and be online if you were rich;

- read some of the many newspapers in both regional languages and English;

- use a telephone—in your own home if lucky, in a store, or at a neighbor's;

- hear and tell stories using some of the ideas in the next chapter. . . . .

Chapter 2

Glimpses of
South Indian Telling

*The true purpose of most Indian storytelling
is to remind listeners of the
true purpose of life: following God.*
T. S. Balakrishna Sastrigal

*Katha Kanchiki, manam intiki.
The tale goes to Kanchi (city), and we go home.*
traditional Telugu tale ending

A great range of tellers still pass on their tales across South India, for many reasons and in many ways. Through the power of storytelling, the gods come to life, morals are taught, history is shared. Through the words of the teller, social injustice is fought, rural development is promoted, politicians gain votes.

Stories are told in theaters, markets, places of worship, at fairs, bus stops, and, of course, in homes. Here are several of today's South Indian tellers and their styles to remind you that just as milk comes first from cows before it fills a carton, storytelling comes first from people before it fills a book.

*Mridangam drum used in
South Indian music and
storytelling.*

Range of Storytelling Styles

Kathaprasangam

While most Indian tellers tell of the gods, in Kathaprasangam, they tell about Communism and much else. This storytelling style, unique to Kerala, was started in the early part of the twentieth century to popularize local Malayalam literature and to fight against the evils of society. While other forms of religious telling have weakened in the state, this secular art has gained strength and now has a true mass appeal.

Audiences in Kerala enjoy political tales by local writers, as well as Russian novels. Tellers often use popular music along with theatrical styles. One popular teller, V. Sambasivan, told in college and as a high-school teacher. In 1975, during the Emergency period of increased censorship, he was jailed and lost his teaching job. Since that time, he has given thousands of programs and taught many the art of Kathaprasangam.

Burra Katha

A teller's words can travel as fast as a newspaper's. So when Gandhi was killed in 1947, the Nittala Brothers created a story, dressed in costumes, added drums and a *tambura* (stringed instrument), then went on stage as *Burra Katha* tellers to share the tragedy. These three teachers from Andhra Pradesh grew very popular and joined the hundreds of other Burra Katha tellers in the state, performing at parties, over the radio, and for the government.

Nittala Brothers telling in Burra Katha style. Photo courtesy Sangeet Natak Akademi, New Delhi.

In the earlier part of the twentieth century, Andhra Communists helped to revive this art form, which grew out of older musical, religious tellings. They found it a style that appealed to the rural audiences they wished to influence. The flexible nature of this style makes it easy to weave information about family planning, better farming methods, or rural sanitation into a longer story of a god or hero. Its use of music, improvisation, and clever dialogue keeps the telling interesting and relevant for city and country listeners today, whether the story is from local history, the great epics, the Bible, or a modern writer.

Chakyar Kuttu and Ottan Thullal

According to legend, a scolding one evening over 200 years ago started another popular storytelling style. That night in Kerala, people say, a storyteller was performing the *Chakyar Kuttu* style in a special *kuttambalam* (temple theater). In this sophisticated, slow-moving style, several verses from the epics are repeated with much embroidery, so in the middle of a long passage, the teller's drummer fell asleep. Much annoyed, the Chakyar storyteller shouted at the drummer, a poet named Kunchan Nambiar. Nambiar went home very insulted and spent the night writing.

The next evening, a new form of telling, *Ottan Thullal*, appeared opposite the Chakyar Kuttu. It was an immediate hit — the teller was more active, the music livelier, the language easier to understand, and the stories full of satire and social comment. The audience abandoned the Chakyar and enjoyed the new form while the drummer enjoyed his revenge.

Today in Kerala, although both forms are still performed, often at temple festivals, Ottan Thullal remains more popular. It travels better, since it can be performed anywhere unlike Chakyar Kuttu, which is found traditionally in temples. Audiences especially enjoy how the gods portrayed in Ottan Thullal seem human and even visit Kerala, while characters from Kerala also travel to the gods.

Two More Styles: Public and Private

A. K. Ramanujan, a noted scholar of South Indian folklore and literature, often described a range of storytelling styles in his native Karnataka moving from *puram* (exterior) to *akam* (interior). He suggested that the puram style of telling, done in public places, often involved props and music, was more elaborate, more practiced, and usually done by men. The akam style, found in homes and courtyards, was quieter, simpler, and usually shared by women (Ramanujan 1991). His ideas offer a fine introduction to these profiles of two tellers, one professional and one not.

◀ T. S. Balakrishna Sastrigal

He speaks seven languages, is an accomplished musician, and can quote about 30,000 poems and proverbs. He knows the major Hindu myths, the stories of South Indian saints, and daily scours several newspapers seeking more tales to pepper his telling. Sri Sastrigal has been telling tales for 40 years, in the very demanding *Harikatha* storytelling style. Yet he looked just like a friendly, modest Indian grandfather dressed in white as he spoke one day in his Chennai home.

"The Indian storytelling forms were made to help people forget themselves in order to remember the true, spiritual purpose of life. Storytelling can transform one," he said, giving examples of the great devotion of older storytellers who could even stop rain for hours while they told.

"Yet much has changed. In the old days, we had all night performances of storytelling. Now we have all night election coverage!" he said with a wink. "And modern audiences are so much more sophisticated and inquisitive. The other day, I told a story about the great demon *Ravana* who has 10 heads. A little boy came up to me later, tugged at my sleeve and asked, 'But sir, this Ravana, supposing he has a cold, what will he do?' "

Sri T. S. Balakrishna Sastrigal performing Harikatha. Photo courtesy Sangeet Natak Akademi, New Delhi.

Sri Sastrigal left his bank job in 1980 to devote himself full time to his calling, and now starts each day at 4 A.M. with puja followed by reading and study. He has traveled throughout India, performing for eager audiences, accompanied by several musicians. But his favorite storytelling times were his beginning programs when he told, alone, in the poorer parts of Chennai. . . . "For with those who lived so simply I felt that I truly shared the real wealth of our land: the strength of our saints and the great spirit of our people."

◀ Indira Seshagiri Rao

She lights the puja lamp, finishes her prayers, then pops *Sesame Street* into the VCR she brought from the United States. Next she picks up and cuddles the toddler she also brought from the U.S. Indira, a kind Indian grandmother, is taking care of this grandson for a year, and telling him many tales, while his parents study in the U.S.

When her own children were small, she started a school in Hyderabad to reach the children of rickshaw drivers. With her energy and spirit, she built it into one of the largest and most respected K-12 schools in Hyderabad, although her goals changed in reaction to the pressures of modern society.

"I wanted to offer children education in their own beautiful Telugu language, to share with them their rich heritage of story and art. But their parents wanted only English to be taught and only English books read. When I gave in and taught through English, at first I found only stories about blond British children to share. So, with my teachers, I worked hard to create materials and to tell tales that would make our children proud to be Indians with Telugu roots."

She succeeded very well, pleasing parents while gently encouraging students to study Indian arts, science, technology; to share traditional tales; and to gather stories from oral history. One such collecting project of Hyderabad's tales even won a coveted prize from the British Council.

Indira's range of stories is vast and she is still eager to share them, but usually in her home now, or while visiting friends. She knows local tales of the fabled Nizam rulers of Hyderabad, as well as South Indian epics like *Silappadikaram*, the well-known story of Kannagi, a faithful wife who avenges her husband's wrongful death. Indira has a story for almost any event, told in a warm style, with small gestures, a quiet voice, and great faith.

Tools of South Indian Telling

Language

◄ Images

A South Indian beauty would not have "golden tresses" but she might have "shoulders like bent bamboo," "a coral mouth," "carplike eyes," and "a lightning waist." Such images, used most often by trained storytellers, provide rich glimpses of South India, past and present.

A famous lullaby from Kerala compares a child to ". . . the peacock dancing with a swaying gait, the melody of the cuckoo's song, the lamp placed in pitch darkness, the breeze bearing the fragrance of flower, the field where goodness ripens, the sweet scented rose water, the magic jewel that I have gained . . ." (Panikkar 1991, 123).

In the epic, *Silappadikaram*, a Tamil city awaits a great festival: "Wooden stands on the balconies of the great mansions were studded with emeralds and gems, with pillars of coral. At the entrance were placed hangings embroidered with sea dragons, and elephant tusks bearing auspicious marks. Strings of pearls swung from large, lovely rings. In the streets, gold vases filled with water had been set out and brass lamps, silken flags, feather fans, scented sandalwood paste, and fragrant flower chains were everywhere to be seen" (Adigal 1965, 22).

◄ Riddles

Riddles also offer imaginative descriptions and metaphors of South Indian life. The usual riddle form is a simple definition as shown below, with "what is it?" understood and not stated.

Water of two colors in a single pot.	*egg*
The red lotus in a black pond.	*lamp*
White earth, black seed, sow with the hand, reap with the mouth.	*writing/reading*
The old woman who eats only wood.	*stove*
A hen that lays 100 eggs as it goes.	*machine*
Golden lock for a small house.	*nose ring*
100 rupee coins in a red case.	*chili pepper*
Handful of rice spread on a blue cloth.	*stars*

Very difficult to share are the rhymes, the alliteration, the poetic meters, the rhythms of the languages a teller would use in South India. Yet using even a few South Indian words can help you explore these cultures. Respect, for example, is reinforced in the Tamil language itself. Verbs have various endings to show degrees of politeness, and words of respect are used when talking to elders, including older brothers and sisters.

Rules of etiquette vary, though, and in many South Indian societies, the use of the phrase "thank you" is not as important as it is in the U.S. Paramasivam explains, "We never use thank you much in words, we show it in our actions. As one of our old proverbs says, 'The left hand should not know what the right hand gives.' We help each other quietly, simply and naturally, without expecting anything or saying thanks out loud again and again."

Names and meanings are also of interest. Many children in South India are named after a god, others after nature or admirable qualities. Here are a few names, along with some useful bits of language to weave into your stories.

Animal sounds in Kannada: *bo-bo* or *owk owk* (dog), *am-ba* (cow),
     ko-ko-ko-ko (rooster)

Counting to five in Tamil: one-nu, rendu, moonu, nalu, anji

Mother, father in Tamil: amma, appa

Tale Beginning in Tamil: *Ore oru urle* (In a certain town)

Muslim Greeting: *As-salaam Alaykum* (Peace Be Unto You)

عَلَیْکُم اسلام

As-salaam Alaykum written in Urdu.

Boys' names	**Girls' names**
Aditya: lord of the sun	Asha: hope
Amir: prince	Basheera: glad tidings
Anand: bliss	Kavita: poem
Gajendra: elephant king	Mala: necklace
Khaleel: close friend	Meena: precious stone
Mustafa: chosen	Mohini: most beautiful
Prem: love	Nisha: night
Ravi: sun	Priya: loved one
Vikram: glorious king	Savita: sun
	Vasanta: spring
	Zeenat: decoration

Gestures

Indian movements are fluid, graceful ones. A street conversation in South India can be a drama rich in action, and a village girl's walk to the well, balancing a clay water pot on her head, is as regal as a queen's.

While some family storytellers use natural actions to tell, professional tellers often train long hours to perfect their gestures. Tellers studying Ottan Thullal, for example, at the famous Kerala Kala Mandalam art center and school, start practicing before dawn: studying voice, Thullal stories, body movement, and *mudras* (hand signs) such as these that help tell a story.

Mudra used in different positions to mean sunset or begging.

Those training in the Chakyar style of telling, in the same state, study first as actors in the oldest living form of Sanskrit drama, *Kutiyattam.* As actors who also do solo telling, they must develop their control of eye muscles and expression to such a degree that, according to master teller Mani Madhavar Chakyar, "you should be able to show the difference between a male and a female moth moving around a flame."

Mudra used in different positions to mean hair, rain, softness, and more.

Music

Stories are often sung in South India: a large and varied ballad tradition is found across the southern region as singers tell tales of local heroes, village gods, troubled spirits, of wrongs by the upper castes against the lower, of women's sorrows. Devotional songs are also woven into telling by professionals and amateurs alike, and at times the audience responds with a set phrase to show interest or joins in a chant.

In the sophisticated Harikatha style, storytellers will often sing in several different Indian languages, and use a wide range of ragas, talas, and musical styles. The collaboration between tellers and musicians in Harikatha is extremely close: a famous teller, the late Sri Embar S. Vijayaraghavacariar, almost stopped telling forever when his brother and accompanist died, declaring that "No one else will ever be able to know just which song from various styles and languages I would want to use at just the right moment. He always did."

Although Indian music is too difficult to explain in brief, musician Annie Penta wrote the notes of raga *Yeman* used in Harikatha for you. "But remember," she warned, "that one cannot really write down the notes for a melody in a raga and have someone play it on a piano with a Western trained idea of pitch. The way of moving from note to note, the strength and duration of the note, the exact tuning are so very important."

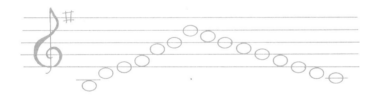

Yeman raga in Western notation.

Instrumental music often enriches South Indian telling, with either the teller or nearby musicians adding mood and emotion through bell sounds (from small brass cymbals, hand held rattles/bells, ankle bells), skillful drumming, or the use of several string instruments.

One of the most interesting instruments used in telling is the *villu* (bow) of the *Villu Pattu* style found at the tip of South India. For this very musical storytelling, a teller sits behind a bow, with bells attached, about 2-meters long. Hitting it rhythmically with a stick, he sings and tells a long story usually during temple festivals. Several others join him—singing, and asking questions, while playing hand cymbals, wood clappers, a drum, or a fine-sounding clay pot (Blackburn 1988).

Sri P. Chinnappa telling in Villu Pattu style. Photo courtesy Sangeet Natak Akademi, New Delhi.

Improvisation, Humor, and Repetition

After Cathy told stories once at a university in Chennai, a professor hesitantly asked, "I liked your actions and language, yet were you really storytelling? You just spoke a few stories to people who didn't know either you or the stories. Isn't storytelling really when you tell a story everyone knows, yet make it new and relevant again?"

Improvisation and repetition are part of the professor's storytelling definition, for they keep some of India's great stories fresh and modern. Since the audience has heard the tale repeated often, a teller can play with it, add to it, embroider it. Repetition is found also as tellers repeat phrases, chants, or refrains both simply and with variations: "she walked gracefully; she swayed gently as she moved; like a swan she walked."

Humor in South Indian telling is shared through plot, characterization, description, and improvisation. Improvisation can be done in various ways; here are three popular techniques that can be sprinkled into storytelling and drama in your own community.

◄ Side Stories and Asides

Weaving in side stories or asides that shed light on a character, setting, or action is the most common technique of improvisation. The side stories might compare a character to someone in another story or on television, a proverb might be added and explained, or a humorous suggestion made. Side stories and comments are taken from works over a thousand years old as well as from today's media. Gurunathan, a young Harikatha teller describing Sita's wedding of long, long ago, brought in very modern times when he said, "Everybody prepared for the big event, but it was difficult to find new clothing because the stores had just had their annual holiday 25 percent off sales!"

Another Harikatha teller, N. Srinivasan, performed in Mumbai (Bombay) when his home state, Tamil Nadu, was suffering from drought, said "That hero performed his puja perfectly, as you must do in Mumbai, since you have water and we don't."

Themes of modern development are also addressed through these side stories and comments. In urging birth control, a teller in Karnataka mentioned how healthy one of the young gods looked. "Why?" he asked the audience, then answered himself, "Because his family practiced family planning and so he was an only child."

However this technique can be tricky to use. T. S. Balakrishna Sastrigal told of a storyteller who went deeper and deeper into a side story. But when he tried to re-join the main tale, he forgot where he was in the story. Quickly he whispered to the drummer working with him, "Where are we?" The drummer, also lost in the side story, replied, "In a marriage hall." This was useless, but luckily the clever violin player quietly helped the teller and the story continued.

◄ Insults

In Chakyar Kuttu, the teller was allowed to improvise insults and criticize his noble listeners. Joseph Kunnath, a story lover from Kerala, described "a Chakyar who wished to remind the king that his ministers were rather dull witted. Thus he told of Hanuman, the great monkey, jumping from rock to rock. As he said, 'And Hanuman jumped from empty spot to empty spot to empty spot,' the teller pointed to each of the ministers' heads, one after another after another."

Even today, gentle insults are given as you can see from Cathy's journal notes:

> ✍ As Paramasivam and I sat eagerly listening to the Chakyar describe Sita's marriage, the Chakyar suddenly noticed me, the only pale face in a sea of sandalwood colors. Pointing my way, he said, "Sita's marriage was so grand that white faces came from far away to attend, even though they didn't understand anything." Everyone laughed, I blushed, and just then Paramasivam decided to take a picture of the audience. As he walked up front to shoot it, the teller's expressive eyes slowly followed him in absolute silence. Right after the camera's bright flash, the teller's hand swept dramatically toward Paramasivam and he cried, "Even big shot photographers came from New York City to steal photos of Sita and Rama." The crowd loved it!

◀ Dialogue and Questions

In Burra Katha, a side teller knows much about contemporary social conditions and uses this knowledge in the telling. He asks questions and makes comments about the story from time to time, making comparisons between the old story and present times. If, for example, the main teller mentions how an old king took care of his people, his companion might say, "Ah, just as today, the government provides free school lunches."

In the Villu Pattu style, the main epic is not improvised; it is "prepared" by repetition and practice, then presented through song and speech. But some of the fast-paced dialogue is changed when needed. This sample from Blackburn's excellent study of Villu Pattu shows the lead singer talking with an assistant about the elephant-headed god Ganesha:

> "*Ah him, he's got a problem.*
>
> How's that?
>
> *Well, have you seen his feet?*
>
> They're big feet.
>
> *And his stomach?*
>
> Looks like a huge vat!
>
> *His head?*
>
> It's an elephant's head.
>
> *What about his ears?*
>
> They're like winnowing baskets."
>
> (Blackburn 1988, 68)

Props

For almost 2,000 years, pictures have been used by Indian storytellers to help tell a tale. The Jains and Buddhists were the first to use paintings, of hell and from the lives of the Buddha or holy ones, as they told stories to strengthen people's faith. Records describing Hindu temple festivals more than a thousand years ago also mention picture showmen, while reports from British civil servants in the nineteenth century describe villages of those who made their living by such telling (Mair 1988).

These visual props can easily be adapted for classroom and library use from roll paper, cardboard, and magic markers.

◄ Chitra Katha (*Picture Story*)

Although the most well known tradition of *Chitra Katha* telling is found near Mumbai (Bombay), tellers using small, hand-held pictures were often found earlier in the Belgaum area of northern Karnataka as well. L. S. Rajagopalan, a fellow story collector, also saw such traveling tellers in the north of his home state, Kerala. They were telling the *Ramayana* at bus stations, using about 20 painted cards, each roughly 30 x 40 centimeters, shown in sequence with the scenes of the story.

Chitra Katha teller. Photo courtesy Sangeet Natak Akademi, New Delhi.

Although this type of picture telling has lost popularity in India, similar forms are found in Japan and now in some parts of the U.S. Everybody likes them; make a set and see for yourself.

Materials and Directions:

eight pieces of uniform-sized white cardboard 6 x 9 inches or larger

one 12 x 18-inch piece of rough paper

pencil and colors: crayons, markers, or colored pencils

1. Choose a story—folktale, legend, true story—with enough action to divide into at least eight scenes.

2. Fold rough paper into eight sections, plan sequence of scenes, then make eight quick sketches of important story scenes.

3.   After you've finished your rough sketches, make illustrations on cards. Since you will be telling the story, too, you don't need to draw every detail. But do use bold colors and a big enough size so that drawings reach out to your audience. Play with the use of close-ups, different viewpoints or sizes, and borders. Number the cards on the back to keep them in order.

4.   Practice your story simply to yourself, adding description, sounds, and character voices as needed. Try tape recording it for feedback. Next, rehearse the story with cards held out steadily, chest high, and story smoothly told.

5.   Now share your tale with listeners, making sure your eyes are on your audience and not the cards. Enjoy yourself and tell your tale again and again and again.

◀ Kalamkari (*Painted Cloth*)

These temple hangings, used earlier to share stories in Andhra Pradesh and Tamil Nadu, are made with natural dyes, buffalo milk, and river water. The cloths vary in composition, usually including the main characters and the setting with a line of story text written at times above the pictures. To make an adaptation for class or library, it works best for small groups of three or four students to make one hanging.

Materials and Directions:

big pieces of newsprint

a large piece of roll paper about 3 x 5 feet

markers

1.   Working in groups of three or four, decide upon a story and make a rough sketch of it on the newsprint. Try one of these common kalamkari formats:
     • Use long rows of boxes with different scenes in each framed box
     • Place major characters of the story in a large middle box with story scenes around it in smaller sections
     • Show only one scene with very large characters to fill the entire hanging

2.   Block out design on large sheet of roll paper, then color using large, easy to see illustrations.

3.   Practice telling in front of finished scroll, taking turns as teller. Remember to use dialogue, improvisation, gesture, music, or sound effects.

4. Hang the story scroll in a well-lit area and use it as a backdrop to your final performance. Point to it as needed (try a flashlight!) and enjoy the well-earned applause afterwards.

Setting

When a storyteller tells as part of a festival, lovely decorations often help to create a festive mood: hangings of folded palm or mango leaves, brass oil lamps, garlands of marigolds or jasmine. If you share South Indian tales, create a setting to enrich the tales. Find a comfortable place where your audience can sit near you on the floor. Try to keep lights relaxed and outside noises dimmed. Serve Indian snacks if you wish, play an Indian music tape to begin, add a few pictures, objects, or a South Indian greeting as a backdrop.

Finally, make some kolams, using colored chalk on outside pavements or magic markers on large sheets of paper inside. Designs based on kolams are scattered through the book to help you, and several more are included below. Share the deep sense of hospitality found in South India as you create beauty to welcome your listeners. Then greet your guests with palms together as you journey with them to a rich land.

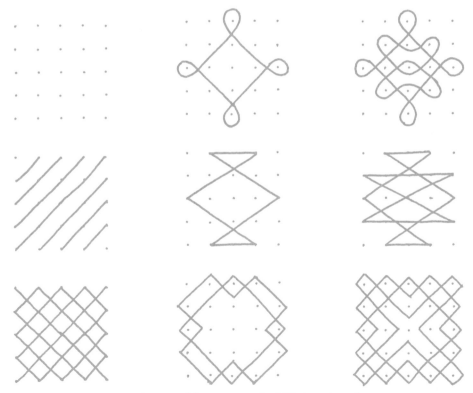

Four simple kolams, each started from top grid of 25 dots then drawn in two stages.

Chapter 3

Value of Simplicity, Problem of Greed

Kannadiyolagina gantigintha kaiyalliro dantu lesu.
Spinach in hand is better than wealth in the mirror.
Kannada proverb

The best richness is the richness of the soul.
Sayings of Prophet Muhammad

Following the example of the saints and sages, many rulers and nobles in South Indian history gave up great wealth to live lives of devotion and discipline. Queen Mahadevi of Karnataka renounced her kingdom to live on dried leaves as she worshipped her god. Kamaraj, a modern leader in Tamil Nadu, wore the same type of white shirt and dhoti everyday as part of his simple lifestyle.

In South India today, people use and reuse materials creatively, thus conserving global resources. Homework papers are recycled into folded bags that are later recycled again. Tires become well ropes, sandals, toys, and more. Old socks may be unraveled to use the yarn again. Leaves are pinned with slender sticks to make thrifty disposable plates, and white cloth scraps turn into potholders, filters, and bandages.

Human nature being what it is, however, the desire to live simply, without pride and greed, must also be nurtured through songs, proverbs, and stories. And perhaps today in South India, with more consumer goods available to buy, along with the problem of corruption, these tales may be more important than ever.

Grinding stone used for making chutneys and grinding spices.

41

Serving with Care

Tiruvalluvar lived in Tamil Nadu about 2,000 years ago and wrote a collection of wise sayings known as the *Tirukkural*. These verses are still quoted and respected today by Tamilians and can even be found on the Internet. Tiruvalluvar dwelt simply with his kind and clever wife, Vasuki Amma, inspiring many others to live with similar care and devotion.

After a long and blessed life, Vasuki Amma grew ill and was about to die. Tiruvalluvar stayed at her side, wishing to do whatever possible for his beloved wife.

"Isn't there some medicine I could bring? Something I could do to make you feel better, even for a while?" he asked.

"There is just one thing," replied Vasuki Amma at last. "Please answer my question so that I can die satisfied."

"Yes, yes, anything."

"Well," she began. "When we were married so long ago, you asked me to put a tiny sharp stick and a small cup filled with water near your rice. For every meal since then I have carefully placed a cup, water, and stick next to your banana leaf. Yet, in all of these years, you have never once used them. Why?"

Tiruvalluvar smiled gently, then spoke. "I wanted to be sure not to waste any food. You see, if you had spilled any rice while serving the meal, I planned to pick it up, piece by piece. Then, after washing each grain in the water, I would eat it to save every bit of rice. But in all these years, each time that you served the rice, you used so much care and patience that you never spilled even one grain. So I never used those things."

At that, his wife nodded with a soft smile of understanding. Soon after, she moved on to another world.

The Greedy Guest

Once in Tamil Nadu, there was a soldier who loved to eat. He found it hard to stop himself, his greed for food was so great. He always ate too much too fast. One evening, he was invited to his captain's home and served a delicious chicken dish. Very pleased, he gobbled down several bites so quickly that he swallowed a bone. The bone stuck in his throat, and suddenly he fainted. His body remained so still that the captain and his wife feared the worst.

"He choked to death," said the wife. "We must move his body right away or someone will accuse us of murder." So the two shoved the body up the steep stairway to their neighbor's home and propped it against the door.

"Help! Someone is hurt!" they cried as they ran home to hide.

At once, a doctor rushed out. But when he pushed his door open, the body tumbled down the steps and landed on the roof of his neighbor, a teacher. Much upset, the doctor stared at the body.

"I can't be seen killing my patients," thought the doctor. "I must hide him." So he pulled the body across the roof until he was over his neighbor's courtyard. Carefully he tied some rope around the body and lowered it down in the dark. The body slid to the ground near a large stone well, and the doctor crept home.

Before dawn, the teacher's wife awoke and went quietly to fetch water. In the dark, she thought she saw her servant sleeping by the well.

"Wake up, lazy girl," said the woman, giving the body a little kick. Because the body didn't move, the woman bent down angrily and started to shake it, shouting, "Wake up and help me!" There was still no response, and when she looked more closely, she saw the person was not a sleeping maid. Instead, he seemed to be a very dead stranger.

"AHHHHHH!" Her scream woke her husband, who rushed to the courtyard.

"I don't know who he is, but he fell on the well and hurt his head," she whispered fearfully, "I'm sure he's dead. We must hide him."

The couple managed to carry the body to a nearby merchant's house. There they leaned him up against a window and fled.

Hearing a noise, the merchant woke immediately. He walked softly through the house, searching for a thief. Then he peeked out the door and saw a man leaning on the window.

"Stop, thief," cried the merchant as he ran up and beat the man. At once, the body dropped down to the ground and made such a noise that the merchant's wife raced out.

"You just killed a man!" she cried. "Quick, let us move him so no one will know."

The two huffed and puffed, pushed and pulled, and brought the body to a street of shops. They left him balanced carefully against a lamp post, then returned home.

Early in the morning, to the sounds of sacred chants, a priest walked to the temple. He was busy praying, his eyes almost closed, when all of a sudden he bumped into something. He heard a thud as a body fell to the ground.

"Oh no," he cried, much upset. "I knocked this poor man down and killed him. Whatever should I do?" As he stood there, confused, some soldiers walked by. Quickly, they pulled the priest and the body to the king's court.

Word of this crime spread faster than smoke into every home. In moments, many townspeople had gathered in front of the palace, including the captain, the doctor, the teacher, and the merchant.

"Our city must be a safe place and a place of justice," said the king to the crowd. "Thus we must punish the wicked man who killed this fine soldier." He looked at the priest and asked, "You were caught right next to the body; what do you say?"

"Sir, I hit this poor soul by accident and ended his life. I stand ready for your judgment," said the priest with his head bowed.

But just then the merchant stepped out of the crowd. "I confess, let him go free," he called out. "I killed the man, thinking him a thief. I beat him and placed his body in the street. I am guilty, not the priest."

Soldiers went to tie the merchant's hands when another cry was heard. "No, he is innocent," shouted the teacher. "My wife and I are to blame. She found him in our house after he fell on our well. Then we tried to hide him." The two stepped towards the king.

VALUE OF SIMPLICITY, PROBLEM OF GREED

"Wait, wait, it is not their fault," shouted the doctor. "I killed him when I pushed him down the stairs last night. Like a coward, I moved the body, and they found him. Let them go. I deserve to die." He pushed his way through the confused crowd and held out his hands. The soldiers moved toward him when suddenly a loud voice stopped them.

"Stop, stop," cried the captain. "He is not guilty, I am. I served the man some chicken and he choked to death on a bone. I was afraid and left him near the doctor's door. Punish me." Stiffly, the captain walked up to the king.

The king looked at all the people claiming to be guilty. He looked at the body, then knelt down next to it. He saw a large swelling near the man's neck. Curious, he pressed the swelling with all of his strength. All of a sudden, with a popping sound, a big piece of chicken bone sprang out of the man's mouth, just missing the king. A cough followed, and everyone watched in amazement as the dead soldier began to move.

"What a delicious chicken," he said, sitting up. "May I have some more?" After he said that, he suddenly noticed that there was no chicken. And he was not at the captain's house. Instead, hundreds of people were staring at him. He stood up and shook his head.

"Why do they all look so shocked?" he wondered. Then he shrugged. "Well, it's none of my business. But I do feel quite hungry. I think I'll go eat." So the soldier started home, dreaming of egg curry, lime pickle, and mounds of rice.

The Greedy Guest

Soma and Bhima

Soma was a very poor man who lived in a small thatched hut. Every morning he went to the forest to cut wood. Every afternoon he sold the wood in the village and bought rice. Every night he had a simple meal with his family, then slept.

One day he was cutting wood close to the river, when suddenly his ax slipped from his hand. It fell into the river, and in seconds it was gone; only ripples floated back to him. He sat down, then started to cry.

All at once, a woman wearing a white sari arose from the river. "Why are you so sad?" she asked.

"I lost my ax," cried Soma. "It is the only thing that keeps me alive. Without it, I can't cut wood, and without wood to sell, I can't buy food to eat. My family will starve."

"Wait," said the woman, and she slipped into the water. She soon returned, holding a golden ax.

"Is this yours?" she asked.

"I'm only a poor man," he said. "How could I have a golden ax? Thank you for trying to help, but that's not mine."

Again the woman went into the water. This time she came out holding a silver ax.

"Is this yours?" she asked.

"No," he said. "I have no money to buy a silver ax."

Pleased, the woman went into the river and returned with his old iron ax. When Soma saw it, he smiled. "That's my ax," he said happily. "Thank you so much."

"You're an honest man, and you don't want more than you need," she said. "Please take all three axes and use them with care." She gave him the axes and disappeared.

Soma returned home overjoyed. He sold the golden and silver axes, built a nice home, and shared his wealth with the poor. But soon Bhima, his greedy neighbor, grew very curious and asked Soma about his new wealth.

VALUE OF SIMPLICITY, PROBLEM OF GREED

Soma happily told Bhima the truth right away. Bhima then wanted more money himself, even though he was already a wealthy landlord. So he ran to the market and bought the cheapest iron ax he could find along with a big, juicy onion.

The next morning, he ran to the forest, found the river, and started cutting wood. After two swings of the ax, he dropped it into the water. Then he took out the onion, cut it, and held it near his eyes, to make him cry. Louder and louder he sobbed until the lady in white appeared.

"Why are you crying?" she asked kindly.

"My ax fell into the water," Bhima said. "How can I support my twenty little children and my mother and father and aunts and uncles now? Poor me. Poor, poor me."

"Wait for a moment," she said and disappeared into the water. When she returned, she had three axes: one gold, one silver, and one of iron.

"Which one is yours?" she asked.

"The gold one, of course," he said. "But since you brought three, give them all to me. I can make use of them." And he eagerly reached for the axes.

"Greediness always brings unhappiness," said the lady, and in seconds she was gone, and all of the axes were too.

Great Wealth, Great Pride

Although Kubera is the god of wealth, his role here has been changed along with his name, as happens in the oral folk tradition. In this tale, he is portrayed as a rich man from the South, rather than a divine being.

Long, long ago, the richest man in India, perhaps the richest in the world, was a man named Kuberan. And he was as proud as he was rich. Kuberan wanted only to flaunt his wealth, never to share it. He threw gold around like water from a jug. His palace of silver and pearls was so big that he sometimes got lost. His wife wore so many gems that she could hardly walk. Still, Kuberan was never satisfied and spent much time finding more ways to show off.

One day he awoke with a new idea. "I will have the grandest dinner in the world and invite only the richest people. I will have so much food that elephant loads will be thrown away as waste. And I must have a very important guest to greet people. Who shall that be?" He thought and thought then suddenly cried out, "Siva. Lord Siva himself. I will ask him."

So he ran to Mount Kailasa where Siva was sitting quietly meditating. Kuberan bowed respectfully and waited. After a while, Siva opened his third eye. "Yes?" he asked.

"Forgive me, great Lord," said Kuberan. "But I am giving a grand dinner and would like you to be my chief guest."

"No, I couldn't," replied Siva. "For I rarely go out any more."

Hiding his disappointment, Kuberan said, "Well, perhaps your lovely wife Parvati could come."

"She likes to stay home as well," replied Siva.

"How about your son Ganesha?" pleaded Kuberan.

Siva agreed to ask Ganesha. Because he loved food, Ganesha eagerly promised to come.

Preparations for the feast took months and months. Huge kitchens were built, then incredible sweets were made from the finest *ghee* (clarified butter) with the richest milk. Ripe cardamoms, the best almonds, and perfect mangoes came from afar. Silk canopies and pearl garlands soon covered the courtyard. On the night of the feast, huge kolams pleased the eye while hundreds of oil lamps burned softly in welcome.

Guests in swirling silks stepped wide-eyed into the great hall to find gold plates and mountains of food. When most of the guests had arrived, Ganesha came, dressed simply and looking quite hungry.

"*Vannakam*," said Kuberan, welcoming Ganesha. He started to introduce him when Ganesha cried, "Later, later. Hurry and feed me first. I'm hungry."

Ganesha quickly sat down and stuffed mango pickle, sambar, and rice into his mouth. "Bring more," he cried. Servants came with mounds of food, but as soon as it touched the plate, Ganesha gulped it down. Again and again, food was brought, only to disappear into his large stomach. "More food, more food. I'm hungry," cried the god. Servants rushed madly to serve him.

Kuberan began to look worried. All of the cooked food was soon gone and no one else had eaten any, yet Ganesha was still hungry.

Bags of raw rice were brought. Ganesha swallowed them all. "MORE, MORE NOW!" he bellowed. Pots of dry grains and banana plants with hundreds of bananas were brought, and he ate everything and cried for more.

Soon all of the food, cooked and uncooked, was gone. Yet Ganesha was still not full. He stood up and chased after Kuberan. "I'M HUNGRY, I'M HUNGRY! FEED ME OR I'LL EAT YOU UP!" he cried.

Kuberan raced through his huge home, looking for something to give Ganesha. Ganesha followed and threw everything he saw into his mouth. Statues, oil lamps, saris, jewels, all were eaten, and still he cried, "I'M HUNGRY, I'M HUNGRY! FEED ME OR I'LL EAT YOU UP!"

Kuberan, terrified, raced out of his now-empty home and saw Ganesha eat the house itself, still demanding more. Kuberan knew only one way to be safe. He ran and ran to Mount Kailasa with Ganesha chasing him, shouting, "I'M HUNGRY. FEED ME!"

At last, Kuberan reached Siva and threw himself down before the great god. "Help me, save me, Lord Siva!" he begged.

As Siva slowly opened his third eye, Ganesha ran up and called to his father, "Appa, he cheated me. He invited me to dinner and didn't feed me enough."

"Is that the problem?" said Siva, looking fondly at his son. "Go ask amma for a small snack."

Ganesha went to his mother and was well satisfied with the tiny sweet she gave him. Siva took one long look at Kuberan, then closed his eyes in meditation once again.

As for Kuberan, he said not another word. He understood now the lesson he had learned. Slowly he stood up and crept back home, a different man. His house was gone, his gold was gone, his great pride was gone, but he had gained the wealth of wisdom.

Chapter 4

Devotion and Faith

One Caste, One Religion, One God.
Sri Narayana Guru of Kerala
(Ayyar 1966, 181)

Thou my mother, and my father Thou.
Thou my friend, and my teacher Thou.
Thou my wisdom, and my riches Thou.
Thou art all to me, O God of all gods.
Ramanuja
(Munshi and Diwakar 1963, 160)

Many stories told in South India encourage a closer relationship between human and divine beings. They tell of devotees, of pilgrimages, of saints like Ramanuja long ago and recent reformers like Sri Narayana Guru. Stories of Siva are popular, while Vishnu appears in stories especially about two of his incarnations (lifetimes) as Krishna and Rama. Kali, Ganesha, and Subramanyam are found often in tales, along with the goddess Lakshmi, who gives wealth, and Saraswati, the goddess of learning. The stories of village deities are spread through local tales and songs, and many temples have their own stories of origin, called *stalapuranas*, which are passed on as well.

A girl saying prayers.

51
DEVOTION AND FAITH

There are also tales of Christian saints, stories from the Bible, and stories about the prophets of Islam. Because the different religions did not always get along, there are tales of disagreements as well, some quite violent, others as restrained as this Hindu-Christian debate:

> The arguments became warm, and Goddess Bhagavati, considering it best to cease further discussions, decamped, and jumping across the Cranganore river, made straight for the temple. St. Thomas, not to be undone, gave chase, and just as the deity got inside the door, the saint reached its outside and setting his foot between it and the door-post, prevented its closure. There they both stood until the door turned to stone (Bayly 1989, 279).

The image of that open door is a fine one to remember while reading the stories that follow—stories that share the range of religious practice and thought in South India past and present.

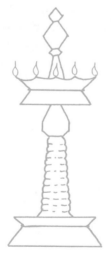

Lives of the Prophets

Children growing up in the Muslim areas often hear stories about the prophets, including the last, Prophet Muhammad, whose life was a most inspiring one. Both of his parents died when he was quite young, and he spent much time alone, pondering and meditating while he worked herding sheep. As he began to preach his ideas, he made strong enemies who tried to kill him, but in the end he brought many people into Islam, and it became one of the world's great religions. Here are two of the many tales of his escapes, which show his kind heart and great faith even in the midst of trouble.

One time Muhammad and his good friend Abu Bakr had to flee from those who wished to kill them. They found a small cave and crept into it. Soon they heard the sounds of searching coming closer and closer.

"We will be discovered at any moment," said Abu Bakr, reaching for his sword.

"No, my friend, Allah is watching," replied Muhammad. "Look at the mouth of the cave."

Abu Bakr watched in amazement as a spider quickly spun a large and intricate web across the cave's entrance. Then a dove came, bringing materials to build a nest. In moments, the nest was complete, right at the cave's opening. She sat upon it peacefully as the spider scurried back and forth in the sunlight.

Just then a voice shouted, "Search that cave; perhaps they are hiding there." The two men pressed into the darkness at the end of the shallow cave. They saw a man glance at the cave and then call out, "No one has been here for ages. There's a spider's web and a nest, all undisturbed. Look elsewhere." After a while, the voices died down. Abu Bakr and Muhammad stayed in the cave a little longer, then continued safely on their way, protected by Allah.

Another time, Muhammad and his companions were returning from a battle when they decided to rest near some trees. Muhammad hung his sword from a branch, then fell asleep underneath it. Soon a nomad came and saw his enemy Muhammad, asleep and unarmed. He grabbed the sword and held it above Muhammad's head, who awoke upon hearing a sound.

"Who will save you now?" asked the nomad, preparing for the final blow.

"Allah alone," replied Muhammad calmly. At that simple statement, the nomad suddenly grew fearful and trembled. The sword slipped from his hand. Muhammad immediately grabbed it and held it to the head of his attacker.

"And who will save you now?" he asked. The man could only shake his head in fear. But Muhammad was generous; he pardoned the man and returned his sword. The man, much impressed by the Prophet, accepted Islam and became a faithful follower from that day on.

Worship of Great and Small

The Christian church, the Muslim masjid, and the Hindu temple were centers of their communities. Great kings built great places of worship to prove their devotion. But many stories remind listeners that the smallest acts of faith are as welcome to the gods as the larger, more visible ones.

In the Tamil city of Thanjavur, the mighty Chola king, Rajaraja I, once ordered construction of a magnificent temple for Lord Siva. As the workers gathered materials and the builders checked the plans, a poor but devout elder woman named Alagi watched with interest. She loved and worshipped the god Siva constantly, so was delighted that a grand temple would honor him in her city.

"I wish I could help in some way," she said to herself. "Yet what can I do?" She thought about this daily as she watched the men building.

One day, she noticed how hot it was under the summer sky. "The poor workers," she said to herself. "The sun is so fierce, those men look so thirsty." At once she knew how she could help and returned to her home. There she mixed together chili pepper, ginger, salt, and water, then added a little yogurt. Happy now, she returned to the building site and shyly offered the refreshing drink to each of the workers. Carefully she poured the liquid into her clay cup, then waited patiently in the heat as each worker drank.

Day after day she went to the site, carrying her heavy clay pot. There was always a smile upon her face as she poured each cup. She never hurried the workers but let each drink at his own pace. She took no drink herself for there was not enough, yet she returned home each night truly content.

Years passed in this way. Then one day she watched the stone-masons work on a large tower. Suddenly she spoke softly to them. "Please, dear sirs, can I make one request? If you need a coping stone for your work, I may have a suitable one in my yard. Please allow me to go bring it."

The workers were delighted to do something for the kind woman who had helped them for so long. They went to her yard themselves and brought the stone. They chiseled it down, and indeed it made a perfect fit. Alagi looked on with great happiness, pleased that her stone could be of use.

Finally the temple was finished. It looked so wondrous that a very special consecration ceremony was planned to open it for worship, with rich offerings, fine music, and special dances to welcome the god. King Rajaraja I, proud of the temple, went to sleep well satisfied the evening before the ceremony. But in his dream, he saw Lord Siva and heard him say, "We are most eager to come and stay in the shelter so kindly provided by Mother Alagi."

Rajaraja I awoke confused and upset from his dream. He called to his ministers.

"Who is this Alagi?" he demanded. "Why did Lord Siva say he was happy with her and not mention me? I have caused this temple to be built. I have brought great riches to raise it up. How did she help?"

No one in the royal court had heard of Alagi, so soldiers went to inquire, and they soon returned with her story. When the king heard of her simple kindness and faith, he felt humbled. He walked to her small hut, then escorted her to the temple, honoring her in front of all.

From that day on, Alagi went daily to the fine, new temple, offering fresh flowers and devotion to Siva. And to this day, people in Thanjavur tell her story to teach their children about faith and to remind them that true worship comes not from giving great things, but from giving with great love.

Druva

========

Harikatha tellers in the south like this tale of single-minded devotion from one so small. The story is well known to many South Indians, as are other popular stories of young devotees, including the Tamil saint Sambandhar who showed his love of Siva at the age of three, and Prahlad, who held on to his faith in Vishnu through many difficult tests.

Long ago lived King Uttanapada, who ruled a large and prosperous land. His two queens, Suniti and Suruchi, each had a son, and the king felt love toward all of his family. However, the younger queen, Suruchi, grew daily more jealous of the first queen. She started to talk against the queen and against her quiet, kind son, Druva.

At first the king did not listen to her. Yet her words, like the cobra's deadly venom, finally entered the king's heart. He gave her more power and did as she wished. Then one day she said in a voice sweeter than sugarcane, "My lord, I have heard rumors. Queen Suniti and her son wish you harm. You must send them away."

As the sun burned with rage at such lies, the weak king agreed. Suniti and Druva were taken to a small hut in the forest and left there. At first they felt great sorrow, alone under the trees. The queen's tears fell like pearls, for she feared the future, and her royal hands felt useless amidst the thorns. But the beauty and quiet of the forest were fine medicines. The young boy grew to love the woods and the animals who lived there. Watching his joy, the queen forgot her pain at times and felt content.

One day, when Druva was seven years old, he ran to his mother and suddenly said, "Mother, who is my father?" She told him of the king, so he asked, "May I go to see him?" Suniti agreed, hoping that a father's love would be shown to his son. Carefully, she dressed him in fine silks carried from the palace. She gave him flowers to present as a gift and took him to the palace gates.

"Now my son," she said. "Remember that you are a prince. Go proudly to the guards and demand to see your father. If the king asks of me, tell him that I love him still. Blessings, my son. Go now. I will wait for you under this banyan tree."

Druva stepped with confidence up to the guards. Word was sent to the king, who invited the boy to enter. Druva walked softly, like flowers falling, up to his father. Eagerly, the king sat the boy on his lap, listening with pleasure to the son he had so missed. But then jealous Queen Suruchi came in.

"What is this boy doing?" she cried angrily. "Send him away at once." The king, afraid of her rage, put Druva on the floor. Druva looked at his father's weak face and the Queen's furious one. He started to walk away, then paused at the doorway, waiting for a word, hoping to be called back. But the king just sat there, looking powerless, and at last Druva left, his eyes fixed sadly on the ground.

"Mother, who is stronger than my father?" he asked moments later. His mother saw the tears in his eyes and said, "Vishnu is the strongest of all, my son. He is called the Lotus-eyed."

"Where does he live, mother?" asked the young boy.

She looked at her son, wondering at his questions. Then she answered carefully, "He dwells in the midst of the forest where wild animals live. It is very difficult to find him; the path to him is full of hardship and not for the young."

Druva said nothing and held her hand as they returned to the forest. They soon slept, but he awoke in the middle of the night. He kissed his mother very softly and tiptoed out of the house. He walked on in the darkness, deeper and deeper into the forest. At last he came to a place where no stars shone, where no moon smiled—a place of shadows and silence.

"Here, surely, is where the Lotus-eyed dwells," thought Druva. "Let me rest and then search further." Soon he slept, but awoke hours later when a low growl sounded near his ear. He saw two burning coals staring at him.

"Are you the Lotus-eyed One?" he asked the tiger eagerly. But there was no answer as the striped beast crept away, shamed by such innocence. Soon a large bear came up to Druva, sniffing. But Druva felt no fear. Instead he asked, "Are you perhaps the Great Lotus-eyed?" The bear could only shake his head and walk away as well. Other fierce animals came and he repeated his question, but they only left, ashamed.

Druva waited patiently, and at last a gentle man came toward him.

"Sir, you must be the Lotus-eyed," Druva said with delight.

"No, I am not," said the man, who was a great sage called Narada. "But I will show you how to reach him. You must say over and over the prayer I will give you." Then he gave Druva a short prayer calling upon Lord Vishnu.

Narada left soon after, and Druva repeated the words of the prayer. Over and over and over he begged the Lord to come. Animals came and circled round him. Red ants crawled upon him. He hardly ate and barely slept. He simply repeated the prayer, day after day, week after week, his mind fixed entirely on Lord Vishnu.

At last one morning, he opened his eyes and saw a glowing figure before him. A kind smile showed on his golden face, and his eyes were indeed like two glorious lotus flowers in full bloom.

"Lord, please take me with you," said the boy, gazing upon Vishnu in great joy. "You are wiser and stronger than my father. Let me be your son."

"My boy, it is not yet time. You must return to your mother who longs for you, then go back to the palace. Your father's heart has changed. You must prepare to be king; your people need you. Later, you will come to me and I will welcome you."

Suddenly the figure was gone. Only the silent dark remained. Druva rubbed his eyes and slowly stood up. He walked back through the woods, holding tightly to his vision.

In her forest hut, the queen sat in great grief, unable to move her limbs, her face like a faded lotus. She thought her son dead and wished only to follow him. Imagine, then, her face when she heard his running steps, when she heard his small call. With wild tears of joy she held him as he told her who he had seen, what he had learned. She gazed at him, her young son, small in size and few in years, but suddenly so wise. Believing his words, she packed their few belongings, and they headed home.

At the palace, the king had indeed learned a lesson. His heart, touched by Vishnu, now welcomed his wife and son as they deserved. Carpets of flowers covered the roads, hangings of rubies and pearls beckoned, dancers and musicians lined the path, brass oil lamps burned brilliantly. The king begged their forgiveness while Queen Suruchi grew ill from jealousy and soon passed away. Her son, kinder than his mother, embraced Druva, and the two grew well together.

After many years, the old king died, and Druva was everyone's choice for king. He ruled wisely, his mind always on the Lotus-eyed. When his hair grew as pale as the white heron's feathers, he gave up the throne. He went to live peacefully in the forest he still loved, praying and offering praise to his Lord.

After he died, there was sorrow in the kingdom until people noticed a new brightness in the sky. For Druva's faith had found its reward. He was released from the cycle of birth and rebirth and welcomed in the heavens themselves. Even today he is seen at night, as a light so bright—seen as the glowing and constant Pole Star in the sky, which shines steadily to remind us of the power of devotion and faith, at any age, in anyone.

DEVOTION AND FAITH

The Great Battle

Hindu gods are many and varied. Forms of the goddess range from gentle ones like Saraswati to the fierce Bhagavati below. The story of Bhagavati and Darika is found especially in Kerala, where it is still dramatically portrayed in dance and ritual. In this story, two important Hindu concepts are used: *tapas* and *mantra*. Tapas is the great sacrifice or penance undertaken to worship a god, in hopes of receiving a blessing or a boon. A mantra is a sacred word or chant that gives power or protection when used.

Long, long ago there was a great and terrible war between the *devas*, beings from the heavens, and the wicked *asuras*. When the asuras seemed to be losing, one of them did great tapas, seeking a boon from the gods. After many hardships, a fearful monster, Darika, was born to her as a reward. At his birth, the sun dimmed, trees crashed to earth, and waves raged through the sea. As he grew in evil ways, he wanted to be the most powerful being in the world and he, too, began to do difficult tapas. Pleased with his devotion, Brahma appeared before him.

"Grant me that I cannot be killed during the day or the night, with stone or iron, inside or outside," Darika requested.

Brahma gave these boons to him and further bestowed upon him two sacred mantras. As Darika left, Brahma offered as well to protect him from a female's rage.

"I need no protection from women," said Darika, laughing at the idea. "Keep that useless boon. No mere female can ever kill me."

Darika's rule began; it was one of too-great power wrongly used. He showed no mercy, only cruelty, and was so full of pride that he insulted and cursed even the great god Siva. Siva's wrath grew until one day it took shape as the mighty many-armed goddess Bhagavati. "Go and destroy that monster," ordered Siva.

The goddess soon found Darika, and a battle began. The earth trembled as they fought and, though their weapons dripped with blood, after many long hours Darika defeated her. Bhagavati returned to Siva, seeking help.

"He has received powerful boons," said Siva. "In order to win, you must discover his secret mantras."

Bhagavati disguised herself as a beggar in rags, broom in hand. She stumbled down to Darika's dwelling and found women there singing hymns and chanting mantras. Wishing to help such a sad-looking woman, they offered rice and gifts to the beggar.

"Dear sisters," said the poor woman, "I thank thee for your kindness. Now I would sit a while and listen to your fine songs. I wish that I, too, could sing such lovely lines."

Pleased by her praise, the women shared the songs and mantras willingly with her. As soon as she had learned them, the beggar left quietly. Returning to her true form, she flew to attack Darika.

Unaware that his secret was known, he marched to fight her, boasting of victory. But this time, although he fought with great strength, he was beaten back. As the mighty goddess attacked again and again, using his mantras against him, his weapons fell and his power weakened. Fearful at last, he fled into the inner room of his fortress.

With red eyes flashing, monstrous teeth gleaming, and fierce weapons in her many arms, Bhagavati pursued him. Yet though he was weary and weak, he was protected by his boons still, so the goddess planned well. At dusk, neither day or night, she dragged him out by his hair. On the doorstep, neither inside or outside, she raised her strong, mighty foot. With the sharp claw of her toe, she pierced the demon's body, thus killing him with neither stone or iron.

Triumphantly, she cut off his evil head and carried it on her sword to Lord Siva. Siva, though pleased to see the monster dead, was suddenly afraid of this powerful goddess. Worried that her glory might equal his own, he spoke to her. "O Great Goddess, your power is needed on Earth. Please go to the sacred land formed by Parasurama, that green, lovely land of rituals and beauty. Live there as the supreme being and be respected by all. You alone are worthy of their praise."

Although she preferred to stay near Siva, Bhagavati followed his wishes and left to dwell in Kerala. And in that rich land she is worshipped still, and her story is danced, sung, and told by many to this very day.

A Tale of Dharma

Dharma—doing one's duty—is important to many in India. The path of dharma is often illustrated through characters like Rama of the *Ramayana* or Yudhishthira of the epic *Mahabharata*. Although people talk of dharma as an idea, in some stories, Dharma also appears on Earth as a divine figure.

After many battles, much bloodshed, and the sorrow of Krishna's death, the great Pandava brothers and Draupadi, their wife, wished to leave Earth and enter Heaven. They carefully handed over their kingdom to those who could rule and gave their treasures away as well. At last one morning, wearing garments of tree bark, the six left their rich palace home.

They walked on as everyone watched with great sadness. Then from the city a little dog ran out and started to follow them. The small group journeyed on, enjoying the company of the friendly dog and thinking of Heaven to come. Days passed in peaceful travel until suddenly Draupadi stopped, weakened, and fell lifeless upon the earth. Everyone gathered around her, hoping to revive her. Only Yudhishthira understood.

"I'm afraid there is no help," he said with grief. "Although she was a very good woman and was a caring wife to us all, she loved one of us more than the others. Her favorite was always Arjuna. Because of that, she cannot enter Heaven as a human." And so, after saying the proper prayers, the brothers and the dog sadly continued on their way.

Next to fall was Sahadeva. Again, the brothers crowded around him, crying and trying to help him. Again, Yudhishthira, their leader and the eldest, spoke. "His sin was to boast too much of his own wisdom. For that he cannot enter Heaven as a human."

On and on they walked until Nakula died.

"He died because he was too proud of his beauty," said Yudhishthira to his two remaining brothers. They went on until Arjuna, the great archer, stumbled and fell. The two last brothers prayed for their beloved friend and companion.

"Why did noble Arjuna need to die, dear brother?" asked Bhima when they finished the rituals.

"Because he bragged that he could kill all the other warriors by himself. He insulted many with his rash words," answered Yudhishthira. Now he, Bhima, and the dog continued. Closer to the gates of Heaven they went until suddenly Bhima fell. Knowing that he, too, was dying, he cried out, "Why, why must I die now? What have I done?"

"Dearest brother," replied Yudhishthira, "although you are a prince of men and have many good qualities, you had the sin of pride. You spoke too often about your strength." In great sorrow, he held his last brother as Bhima's eyes closed. Then, feeling most alone, Yudhishthira said the final prayers for a brother well loved.

Finally, with only the little dog next to him, Yudhishthira saw ahead the gates of Heaven. All at once, a glowing chariot came from beyond those gates. In it sat Indra, the king of Heaven.

"Come now into Heaven with me, O mighty Yudhishthira," said Indra.

"Great Indra," said Yudhishthira, "I have lost my brothers and dear Draupadi. How can I enter Heaven without them?"

"Do not fear," answered Indra. "They are already in Heaven, awaiting you. Due to their sins, they had to leave their human bodies to enter Heaven. But because of your fine qualities, you have the honor of entering Heaven with me right now, in your human form."

"I thank thee," said Yudhishthira, "for this great reward. I will gladly come now." And he called to the little dog, telling him to jump into the chariot.

"But you must leave the dog, as you left your brothers and Draupadi," said Indra. "He cannot come with you now."

"I left them only after they died," replied Yudhishthira. "But this dog lives. I cannot desert him and leave him alone."

"A dog cannot enter Heaven," said Indra. "Leave aside that little animal and come now."

"I have always given shelter and food to those who asked. I have always protected those who trusted me, helped those who needed help. That is my duty, my dharma. How then can I leave this small dog who has been my faithful friend?" argued Yudhishthira.

"You are speaking foolishly. The dog is not worth your worry. Come now."

"If the dog cannot come with me, then I shall stay with him," said Yudhishthira. "Please go now, for I cannot leave him, that is certain. If I did, I would leave as well the path of dharma."

All at once, the dog's body disappeared and in place of the dog stood a radiant figure, that of Dharma himself, Yudhishthira's father.

"My son, I am proud of you," he said. "You have proved that you are the son of Dharma. You have earned your place in Heaven. Go now with joy and see those you love."

Thus, with great happiness, Yudhishthira entered Heaven and joined all who awaited him there.

What Is Real?

In South India, as everywhere, there are those who take advantage of people's faith and their desire to believe. This warning tale comes from Kerala, where science, communism, and religion manage to coexist creatively.

Once a *guru* lived on a remote hillside in Kerala. One day a man came to him, asking to be his disciple. The two talked daily about life, worship, belief. Every day they prayed and performed rituals, living very simply with only one change of clothes for each.

Months passed in this quiet manner until at last the guru said, "I have taught you many things, and soon you must leave me. Before you go, we will visit the outside world, to prepare you." So they walked down from their calm forest shelter into a bustling town where they saw a poster for a political meeting.

"Let us attend this meeting to hear the speaker," suggested the guru. So they went and mingled in the crowd, watching and listening. The politician told the people all the wonderful things he would do for them, then finished by saying, "Because you have water problems, I promise to put in twenty more water pumps here." His words received great cheers, and afterward he hurried to another meeting. At that place, an old school building stood ready to collapse. So he ended his speech by saying, "I promise to repair this school and make it a great model of education." Then he raced on to one last meeting in an area with little electricity. There his cries filled the air with hope, and as everyone clapped, he promised to bring in more lines for electrical power. Pleased with himself, he started back home.

"Let us follow him," said the guru. They went to his house, a good house in a nice location. Hiding, they listened outside a window as the politician's wife brought him tea and asked about the meetings.

"People liked me," he boasted. "I think I will get re-elected. When I do, I'll select a corrupt contractor to do the water pumps and electric lines, then demand a big bribe. We'll use that money to buy jewels and have a grand marriage for our daughter. Next, I'll find another cheat to do the school repairs. He can order extra materials for the school but use them instead to make this house bigger."

Outside, the guru motioned to his disciple and they moved away. "Now you see what is real," said the guru as they walked home. "He sounded so good in the meetings, but the truth is different." They returned, slept, and did their morning rituals. Now the guru had one thing left to do. He called his disciple and spoke.

"As you saw last night, many people think first of their own needs and act selfishly, just as the politician sounded honest but was really thinking only of himself. Even so, I myself have been thinking only of my needs. I committed a crime years ago and came here to hide. I knew that after sixteen years, the law could not touch me and I could not be arrested for that crime. Now there is only one more day left to complete my sixteen years. Tomorrow I will be free. I will leave these woods, give up this disguise, and gamble everyday in the big city. Finally, I can say what I think and won't have to pretend any longer. I'm amazed that I fooled you for so long."

The eyes of the disciple grew large as he stared at the guru.

"Guru, what I saw yesterday and what you just said are very clear lessons to me," he said. "So now I must tell you my truth as well and speak of my needs, for I too am selfish. I have been working for the government for a long time. I have a wife, children, and many expenses. Last year, my boss told me that if I did what he asked, he would give me a promotion with a pay raise. I agreed, and although it took a long time searching, at last I came here to you."

All of a sudden, he pulled out handcuffs and slapped them on the guru.

"You see," he finished, "I am a police officer, and my boss said that if I bring you to the judge today, I will be promoted." With a satisfied grin, he took the false guru to jail and soon received his promotion. Thus he proved that in religion, as well as in politics, things are not always what they seem.

The Right Time

The law of *karma* declares that actions in one lifetime build up and, good or bad, affect a future lifetime. Doing good bears the right fruit, even though it may take time, while wrong deeds cause negative effects. In this little tale, the idea is spelled out very simply.

Once a man walked through the woods on a dark night. All at once, a bell's soft ring brushed his ear. He heard a voice chanting prayers, and he smelled sweet incense. Curious, he went closer and saw a man dressed in the robes of a holy wanderer. The man sat worshipping before an altar, begging the goddess to show her face.

"Please come and speak to me, your devotee," he prayed. "For many years I have been faithfully praying to you. Grant me one glance of your holy face."

Suddenly a face did appear—the face of a hungry tiger, who pounced upon the devotee, killing him at once. The second man, hidden behind a tree, waited until the tiger was gone. Then he came out and, seeing the bell, the fruits, the flowers still ready for worship, he sat down. Curious, he picked up the bell and rang it to hear the sound. Immediately, bright light turned the dark forest into day as the goddess appeared.

"Ask a boon of me, my devotee," she said gently. "I am pleased with your worship."

"No, no," he said at once. "There is a mistake. I only sat down here and touched the bell. I have never worshipped you in my whole life. But the man who just died had been trying for years to see you. He is worthy of your visit, not me. You are too late."

"No, I am not," said the goddess. "You have only forgotten your previous lives. The man who just died will be reborn in a better life. His prayers will be rewarded in that way, because he only started his worship. But you have undergone great hardships for me, again and again. You have worshipped me for many lifetimes. Thus you were born with the good earned from the past, and a touch of the bell now was enough to bring me to you."

Telling the Future

On some South Indian streets, one can find men surrounded by charts and diagrams, eager to tell the future, or see trained parrots pick out a fortune from colorful cards. Through special calendars, one can foretell the proper time of day for various actions and avoid inauspicious times. Sometimes, as in this tale, small details can cause great changes in such predictions.

Once the queen of a southern land was about to give birth. Her husband arranged for a famous and wise astrologer to write the child's horoscope. The astrologer came to stay near the queen so that he could calculate the horoscope at the exact moment of birth. Calling to the queen's faithful servant he said, "Take this lemon, and throw it out the door the second the child is born. It will come rolling right to me, for I will sit waiting outside. As soon as I see it, I will make the horoscope. That way, we will be certain to have the correct timing for a perfect reading of the stars."

Several days later, the queen gave birth to a lovely little boy, and a lemon came rolling to the astrologer. He immediately made the horoscope and was relieved to find it a good one.

"Great king," said the astrologer as he presented it to the king. "Rest assured that your son's fate is a fine one. He will grow to become an honest and wise ruler."

"I am well pleased for my son," said the king, and he rewarded the astrologer with much gold and a costly silk shawl.

Years passed, and the boy grew up not to be wise, but foolish in a sneaky way. He was not at all honest, but rather a young crook, always lying to everyone. The king watched, sadly puzzled by the boy's behavior, waiting for the child to change and follow his horoscope.

Yet the lazy, dishonest boy only grew up into an even more lazy cheat and scoundrel. He could never be a ruler, that was certain; the kingdom would be ruined in weeks. So, although the king managed to keep his son out of trouble, he remained confused when he recalled the boy's promising horoscope.

At last the king sent for the wise astrologer. "I was so pleased with your horoscope years ago," said the king. "And I know that your predictions are usually correct. Indeed, you are the best astrologer in the land. Can you tell me, then, what has happened to my son? Why were you so wrong about his future?"

"Sir," replied the astrologer, "I, too, do not understand. I have watched your son grow, and I know now that the horoscope that I wrote was for another child. Your son will not change. But where was my mistake? I wrote the horoscope as soon as the lemon reached me. Perhaps we should ask the queen's servant what happened that day."

The old woman was called and came in slowly, carrying her years carefully.

"Try to remember the birth of my son," said the king kindly. "And tell us what you did then."

Although nervous, the woman spoke firmly. "I stayed with your wife, oh king, helping until the moment of birth. As soon as the child was born, I picked up the lemon and tossed it out the door. But there was a small doorstep blocking the path. The lemon hit it and rolled back to me, although I didn't notice. I prepared the baby and took care of the queen as well. After some time, I suddenly saw the lemon. I picked it up and threw it again. On this second try it rolled right to the gentleman waiting outside."

"That explains it," said the astrologer. "There was a delay that I did not know about. Thus the horoscope I wrote was for someone born later than your son. Someone blessed by the stars. I truly wish that your son was that one, but we cannot change the message of the heavens." Then the astrologer bowed as he left. And although he felt truly sorry for the king, he was much relieved that the stars had not lied.

Color
Photographs

Man of the Toda people, in front of his home in Nilgiri hills, Tamil Nadu. © Lou Corbett.

Whole streets are covered with colorful Kolams for the Pongal holiday, Tamil Nadu.

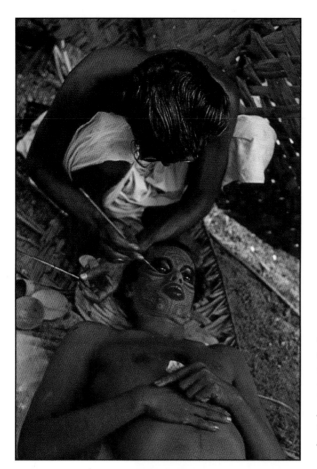

After an actor has sung ballads of a hero or god, make-up of natural colors is applied to help transform him into a hero or god during Teyyam festival, Kerala.

These intricate hand puppets based on the famous Kathakali dance drama have recently been revived with the help of artist G. Venu, Kerala.

Muslim Masjid in Kerala. © *Lou Corbett.*

One of Kerala's many beautiful backwaters.

A village girl enjoys a clever homemade swing in Andhra Pradesh. © Lou Corbett.

Crowded temple cart procession in a city festival of worship in Madurai, Tamil Nadu. © Lou Corbett.

Games are many and varied in the South. This tricky balancing game is about to end in Tamil Nadu. Photo courtesy of Raghauendra Rao.

Many South Indian children work to help their families; here a boy repairs the family fishing net along the Tamil Nadu coast.

Women at village well in Andhra Pradesh. © Lou Corbett.

Huge boulders near Hampi, Karnataka. © Lou Corbett.

Close-up of a Teyyam with crown, headdress, and weapons, Kerala.

A hand painted crown made from inner tree lining and used for a night's ritual, Kerala.

Temple and landscape near Hampi, Karnataka.
© Lou Corbett.

Bright South Indian flower from Kanataka.
Photo courtesy of A. D. Edward Raj.

Chapter 5

Respect for Family and Elders

If you have some problems, you can go to the elders. There are many people to help you in our families. And you learn to be unselfish; I think that is good and healthy.

G. Saraswati, Chennai

He who wishes to enter paradise must please his father and mother.

Sayings of Prophet Muhammad

The family remains strong in South India. Younger children and babies are often held; older children are expected to obey parents and elders; and adult children show much respect for their parents. In the past, the extended joint family was common, with elder parents, their children, and grandchildren sharing a home. Although this is changing in many areas to smaller nuclear families, relatives will still gather for festivals, weddings, and the many rituals of the life cycle.

An extended family brings both comfort and tension, just as children bring both happiness and pain. However, sons may still be more welcome than daughters, because they perform the Hindu ceremonies when their parents die. Sons also can ask a sometimes considerable dowry for marriage, which puts the bride's family at a disadvantage. Yet even through the challenge and changes of today, family values continue to be passed on through stories such as these.

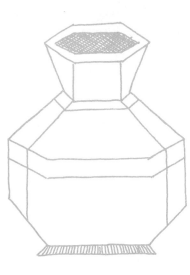

Pot used to boil water or grains.

Who Will Win

Siva, the wise father of Ganesha, once called to his two sons, suggesting a small contest. "I will give this sweet to whoever goes around the world the fastest," he said, holding out a large, delicious milk sweet.

Subramanyam, Ganesha's brother, knew the prize would soon be his. For he could fly swiftly in his chariot, circle the Earth, and be back in only hours, while his big, clumsy brother Ganesha would take almost forever. Bidding farewell to his parents, Subramanyam set off happily.

Ganesha thought for a moment, then smiled and began to move. His large elephant head, with its heavy trunk, did slow him down, but he did not have far to go. He simply walked carefully around both of his parents.

In a few minutes he had circled them and stood respectfully in front of his father once again, his great head bowed.

"Father, please give me the prize," he said.

"But you did not go around the world; you stayed here," replied Siva.

"Yet, father," argued Ganesha, "the prize is for he who goes first around the world. I have just done that. You see, my parents are indeed the whole world to me."

His parents smiled, well pleased. Much later, Subramanyam returned home and claimed the prize. But the sweet was all gone, so he went to sleep a bit hungry and perhaps a bit wiser.

A Devoted Son

Long ago, a kind only son named Shravan worked hard to help his parents, who were both blind. He tried to provide all that they wished and never worried about his own needs. And as their hair grew whiter than the clouds, they longed to bathe in the sacred river Ganges.

"I wish so much to visit that great river," sighed the father. "If we die near those holy waters, we would surely have a better life next time."

This dream seemed impossible to grant; they would need much help to go so far. But Shravan couldn't refuse their wish. He looked at the two tenderly and decided to carry them himself. He made a strong carrying pole that he could hold in the middle. From each end, he suspended a large basket. When he was ready to begin, he gently placed his mother in one basket and his father in the other. He picked up the pole, balanced it most carefully on his shoulder, then slowly began to move.

As he walked, he described the land they traveled through. "I see crows resting on quiet cows. Over there are water buffaloes cooling in the mud," he said. "Can you hear the wind in the palms? It makes them bend like dancers."

His parents listened eagerly to his words and to the new sounds of the journey. In this pleasant way, they traveled toward the Ganges.

One evening, they stopped in a quiet forest to shelter. After the night's sleep, Shravan awoke early and went to the nearby stream to fill a water jug for his parents. Now at that time there was a young prince, Dasaratha, hunting in the same forest. He was a fine hunter, but one too proud of his skill. He enjoyed boasting of one technique he had perfected.

"I can hear a sound from afar, know what animal it is, and where it stands," he bragged to his friends that day. "Then with a single shot, I can bring it down." Soon after he spoke those words, the prince called out, "Listen. I hear an elephant in the woods there, drinking water."

Pointing at a distant tree, he sent an arrow flying at the elephant. Suddenly a dreadful but very human cry of pain tore through the air. He ran to the sound and found a young man lying by the stream, with an arrow in his chest.

"Noble sir," the young man gasped, "Why did you kill me? What harm have I done you? Who will look after my parents waiting for me? Who will give them this water?" With such sorrowful questions, he lost strength and soon died in the prince's arms.

Dasaratha, full of grief and shame, gazed at the young man's face as he laid him gently down. Then he picked up the jug, still full of water, and understood his terrible mistake. With mournful steps, he carried the jug toward the parents. When he saw them, waiting eagerly for their son, he stopped.

"Come quickly, my child," cried the father. "We hear the water you carry. Why do you stop? Hurry, we have missed you. You are our eyes and our life."

The young prince forced himself to go and kneel before them.

"Wait. Who are you?" demanded the father. "Your steps are not those of our son. Where is he? What has happened?"

"Forgive me if ever you can," said Dasaratha, and told them what he had done. "I can never forgive myself, but I promise that you will always be given the best care. I will be as your son."

Sobs shuddered through the mother while the father sat stony cold and furious. At last he spoke.

"We do not need your charity. We can never forgive you. And I curse you. My curse is that you, too, will know the unbearable pain of losing a son. Yes, you will die as I will, from great grief and sorrow, separated from the son you hold so dear." With those words, the father turned from the prince and comforted his wife, both of them eager only for the blessing of death.

As for Dasaratha, years later when he was a famed and powerful king, he was forced by a vow to send his beloved son, Rama, into the forest for fourteen long years. When Rama left, the king knew such great sorrow that he grew deathly ill and recalled the angry words of Shravan's father. Soon after, with Rama too far away, Dasaratha did die of grief and sorrow as the curse of another father came true at last.

Strange Fruit

Problems between in-laws are shared through stories, songs, and gossip. Many South Indian marriages, however, are within a large family and community network, so the bride doesn't marry a total stranger; thus problems can be less severe in parts of the south. In this tale from Kerala, the daughter-in-law has more power than the mother-in-law at first, but then. . . .

Once a woman lived with her husband, her mother, and her mother-in-law. Harmony did not dwell in this home, for the wife always favored her mother, and both women bullied the mother-in-law. Every day the wife served her mother the most rice, the best mango pickle, and the sweetest banana, but gave only scraps to her mother-in-law. Every day, the wife's mother sat on the cool porch but ordered the mother-in-law to weed the garden, feed the chickens, and grind the spices. Day after day this went on, until the mother-in-law was so weak and tired that she wished only to die. She had no strength to stand up to the two women, yet hated to bother her son. Because he traveled so often for work, he never knew how his mother suffered.

One day, the wife made some rich, milky tea for her mother but served only water to her mother-in-law. When the poor old woman gently asked for a sip of tea, her daughter-in-law shouted, "We do so much for you, and all you do is complain. Get out of this house if you don't like it here!" She picked up a big stick, shook it at her mother-in-law, and chased her out of the compound.

Very frightened, the woman stumbled toward a nearby Kali temple. She stopped to gather forest flowers, then placed them before Kali's statue. "Mother Kali," she whispered, "Forgive me for offering such poor flowers. I wish to give you much more, but I have nothing. Please, since you help so many, help me now. My daughter-in-law and her mother are so cruel. They feed me only scraps, make me work so hard, even hit me. I am desperate. Let me die so that I can have a better life next time."

From the image of Kali suddenly came a voice. "Do not be sad. I will help. Stay with me tonight, and in the morning you will find a fruit here. Eat it and your fortunes will improve."

Much relieved, the woman spent a peaceful night in the dark temple, worshipping Kali and singing her praises. In the morning, when she awoke, she saw a lovely fruit. She picked it up with a prayer of thanks.

Meanwhile, early that morning when the son returned from a trip, he found his mother missing. Very much afraid, he ran seeking her. At last, he reached the Kali temple and saw her walking away from it, holding a fruit in her hand. Eagerly, she told him about her night's stay and the promise from the goddess. Her son urged her to try the fruit, so she slowly ate it. Yet nothing happened.

"Climb on my back, mother, and I will take you home. Things will be better there, I promise," said her son. She wrapped her arms around his neck and they set off. But as they walked, he noticed her feet start to change. They seemed to grow younger, to look smoother. And the body he was carrying started to feel different—stronger and full of energy. When he returned to his home, someone hopped quickly off his back. He turned and saw a fine, young-looking woman who smiled with the confidence of youth.

"What happened?" cried his wife. "Did you find your mother? And who is she?"

"She is my mother," said the man happily, and he told of Kali's help.

The wife was extremely jealous and ran to her mother. "Go quickly to that Kali temple and pretend to be unhappy," she told her. "Then you'll get a magic fruit to make you young. And ask for some jewels and gold for me too."

With a greedy grin, the old woman hurried to the temple. Just before the door, she picked a few scraggly weeds and threw them down in front of the image. Then she sat down and started to complain.

"Ah, Mother Kali," sighed the old woman, "I have so many problems with my daughter. Much more than that spoiled woman you saw last night. She's a liar, she has an easy life. I eat only old rice mixed with sand. My terrible daughter makes me work in the hot sun and beats me if I try to rest. She is heartless. My life is worth nothing. Let me die here."

Kali's voice sounded in the temple. "Poor woman. Stay with me tonight, and in the morning you will find a fruit. Eat it and something will change."

Satisfied, the old woman spent a long, hard night in the temple, dreaming of her soon-to-come youth. She said no prayers but only muttered and complained all night of the bugs, the cold, the dark, the dust—everything.

"At last," she cried when she saw the sun. "Now I can leave this smelly place if that silly goddess has kept her word." She looked down and saw a fruit. "Well, I fooled her," thought the woman, chuckling. Quickly, she gobbled the fruit down. Just then, her daughter came looking for her.

"You still look the same, mother; the fruit must take a while to act. Get on my back and we'll go home," she said. So the old woman climbed on her daughter's back. As they walked, the daughter felt her mother grow heavier and heavier. She felt something soft rub against her back. Suddenly, she looked down and saw that her mother's feet were hard, tough, and strangely shaped. Right before the house gate, she felt something kick her, then leap off her back. She turned to look and heard the great, noisy bray of a donkey. The fruit had done its work. There stood her furry mother on four legs with two big, floppy ears.

From that day on, things were different in that house. The young wife was now respectful to her mother-in-law. She served her fine food and never made her work hard, for the mother-in-law was strong and could well defend herself. And if ever the wife felt like speaking back, complaining, or losing her temper, she just looked over at her mother, the donkey, and kept her mouth tightly shut.

My Son, Your Son

In large, extended families, children can be raised by several mothers and fathers, unless something happens to create a separation. . . .

Once two brothers, Gopal and Vasu, lived in one house with their mother and their wives. After a while, a son was born to each couple, and the home was happily noisy. The family worked well together most of the time, and the two boys felt loved by every adult. In fact, the boys often thought that they each had two sets of parents, not one. But then one day, Gopal brought home two guavas and called to the two boys.

"Here is one for each," he said and held out two hands. He carefully gave the bigger fruit to his brother's son, saying, "This is for you." Then he gave the smaller one to his own son, saying, "And this is for you."

From the porch, his brother Vasu watched. The next day, Vasu and his wife packed their things and started to move out of the house. Much alarmed, Gopal ran up to his brother.

"Why are you leaving?" he asked.

"My brother," said Vasu, "I am leaving because you gave the biggest guava to my son."

"Why does that make you go?" asked Gopal in confusion. "I thought you would be pleased that I gave your son a bigger fruit than my own son."

"No," sighed Vasu. "I am not happy. I feel sad and sorry that you did that. Before, I always felt that both of our sons were the same to both of us. That we loved them and treated them equally. I always felt that I had two sons, not one. Now, even though you were kind, I see that to you, there is a difference between the boys. I am afraid that the longer we stay, the more you will feel this difference, and then your behavior to the boys will change. We will leave now but visit often. We will live nearby and help you always, yet now we are two brothers with two families, not one family all together."

RESPECT FOR FAMILY AND ELDERS

A Teacher's Skill

In the traditional Hindu teachings, the *guru* (teacher) was much respected. Students often went to quiet *ashram* schools to serve and study with a guru. In modern South India, although school standards and supplies vary greatly, teachers are still respected and obeyed.

A young man once went searching for a guru to teach him special skills. At last he heard of a sage known for his powers, who lived by the great Meenakshi temple in Madurai. The young man hurried to the temple, but when he saw the teacher, he was most upset. For the man, sitting in clothes so patched and mended, seemed to come from the poorest house and the lowest caste. "However, he may know some magic," thought the young man. "Let me see." He bowed before the teacher and became his disciple.

The teacher was indeed wise, and, before sharing his great knowledge, he tested the man by teaching him several tricks. As the studies grew harder, though, the young man grew bored with them. He left the teacher and started to roam, impressing people with his new tricks. At last he was called before the king of Varanasi, a holy city of the north.

"I have heard of your talent," said the king. "On the street, my minister saw you bring a summer mango from the air in the midst of winter. I wish to see this wondrous skill myself."

The man bowed eagerly, knowing that his fortune would soon be made. Then he slowly stood up, reached high in the air, shook his hand three times, and suddenly held a mango.

"Marvelous," said the king. "You must tell me the name of your teacher. Then make one more mango for the queen, and you will be richly rewarded."

But the young man had become too proud in his travels. He was now ashamed of his teacher and regretted learning from a poor man of such a low caste. So he lied and gave the name of another famous saint. Satisfied, the king nodded, then asked for a last mango.

"With pleasure," said the young man. "Here is a mango perfectly ripe and ready for the queen."

Smiling, he reached up as usual with a flourish, then shook his hand three times, ready to grasp a mango from thin air. But nothing came. He tried again, but still no mango was seen. With a frightened frown, he tried over and over and over. But he held only air each time. No mango ever appeared. At last, he left the palace in disgrace, to the sound of jeers.

He wandered for years after that, trying again and again to make a mango appear. But never again was he able to do even the simplest of the tricks he had learned. His knowledge had vanished and returned to its source. For without respect for your teacher, nothing is possible.

Chapter 6

Hospitality and Friendship

Kshama balam.
Patience is power.
Malayalam proverb

The Western notion of individualism—the idea
that the person has an identity separate from
others and has a right, nay, an obligation to act
as an autonomous person—is considered
selfish by most Indians even today.
(Mines 1994, 3)

In South India, children are taught to think of others first—to consider the needs of family, community, and nation while learning the values of sacrifice, patience, and generosity. As a result, hospitality is ever-giving, self-sacrifice is expected, and close friendships last for years.

Will this continue in the future? In the *Times of India* newspaper, on August 16, 1987, an old folktale took on contemporary dress as it described a modern lawyer who had helped his friend through a difficult lawsuit. The friend thankfully gave the lawyer a fine leather wallet. The lawyer, much annoyed, said that friendship and a wallet alone would not cover his fee of 500 rupees. At that, the friend took the wallet, pulled out 500 rupees

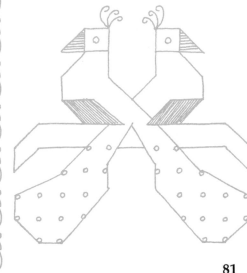

from the 1,000 rupees inside, then gave the wallet back with only 500 rupees left.

Perhaps such modern economic ambition will change traditional values, as some Indians suggest. Perhaps not, if the right stories are told often enough. . . .

Parrots sitting together in
a kolam design.

Yes Dear, Do

Here is a very tellable tale that proves how help and friendship can come from unexpected places.

Long ago in South India, a girl named Priya grew up and married Hari, a kind merchant. The couple lived peacefully with Hari's mother, but although all three worked very hard, they never had much to eat. So one day Hari said sadly to Priya, "There is not enough work here, Priya. I must go far away to earn some gold. Take care of my mother; treat her as your mother; help each other. I will return as soon as I can."

Priya tried to stop him, but he had to leave. She wrapped lemon rice, mango pickle, and her love in a banana leaf for him. His mother blessed him and cried softly after he left.

The two women cleaned, cooked, and stitched as before, but now the mother always seemed sad. Priya wondered how to help, how to make her stop missing her son. One day, Priya had an idea. She would ask the mother questions, all of the time, to keep her mind busy. She started right away.

"Amma, shall I sweep the floor?" Priya asked.

The mother looked up and forgot her worries as she answered, "Yes dear, do."

Priya swept and soon asked, "Amma, shall I make tea now?"

The mother again forgot her sadness as she replied, "Yes dear, do."

After tea, Priya asked, "Amma, shall I clean the pot?"

"Yes dear, do," answered the mother, distracted from her sorrow.

Priya kept on questioning, and the mother soon had no time to worry because she was so busy making replies.

"Amma, shall I go to the market?" "Yes dear, do."

"Amma, shall I light the oil lamp?" "Yes dear, do."

Even, "Amma, shall I go to the bathroom?" "YES dear, DO."

Question followed question and year followed year. Hari still had not returned. One day his mother, who was now quite old, became ill. Priya nursed her gently, but the older woman grew weaker and weaker. One day she spoke softly to Priya. "My dear, I have lived a long and good life. It is time now for me to leave. Take care and wait for my son."

"No, you cannot die. You can't leave me alone," begged Priya.

"I must," said the mother. "You will be fine."

"No, I will be too lonely. You are my only friend. Who will answer my questions?"

"I know you only asked them to help me," said the mother. "And they did. Thank you. But you always knew the answers." Yet Priya cried and felt so sad that at last the mother reached behind her pillow and pulled out a doll carved from rosewood. She gave it to Priya.

"Take this, then, Priya. It will help. When you miss me and want to ask a question, ask the doll. Let her be your friend." Then the old woman smiled weakly, closed her eyes, and changed worlds.

Priya's tears tumbled down upon her faded sari for hours until at last she picked up the doll. She stared at it. Although it was only wood, it felt good to hold.

"Doll," she said slowly. "Should I prepare the body for the death rituals?"

And the doll said, "Yes dear, do."

So Priya did what was needed and soon she sat alone in the house. She picked up the doll and said, "Doll, shall I make us some tea?"

And the doll said, "Yes dear, do."

Priya did and felt better, so she asked, "Doll, shall I sweep the floor?"

The doll said, "Yes dear, do," and Priya did.

Next Priya asked, "Doll, shall I cook the rice?"

"Yes dear, do."

"Shall I grate the coconut?" "Yes dear, do."

"Shall I go to the bathroom?" "YES dear, DO!"

Days sped by, and Priya felt less lonely with her friend the doll. Then one afternoon, as she started to cook sambar soup, she saw that the fire needed feeding. But there was no wood left in the house.

"Doll," she said, "we need wood. Shall we go gather some in the forest?"

The doll said yes, so Priya tucked the doll into her sari and set off across the rice fields. In the forest, Priya gathered dead branches and soon had a big bundle balanced on her head. But it was now very late and the banyan tree, wrapped in shadows, rattled its leaves. Priya trembled as she searched for the path home.

"Doll," she whispered at last. "It's so dark and I'm lost now. Shall we stay the night in a safe tree and go home in the morning?"

The doll said, "Yes dear, do." So Priya hid the wood, held the doll, climbed up a sturdy tree, and at last fell asleep. Her soft snores sang through the night until suddenly she heard loud cries.

"THAT'S MINE!"

"NO, IT'S MINE!"

"MINE!"

Priya looked down and saw shining coins heaped like coconuts in the market. Fighting over the coins were three fierce-looking robbers. Priya knew if they found her they would kill her at once. What could she do? She picked up the doll to give her courage. She tried to think, but her fingers shook so badly that she dropped the doll. It fell straight down and hit the biggest robber right on his bald head.

"HELP!" he cried. "THE SOLDIERS HAVE FOUND US. THEY HIT ME. RUN!"

The three raced off, leaving all the gold behind. Still scared, Priya waited and watched, but hours passed and they didn't return. When at last the morning sun smiled through the leaves, she felt brave enough to slide down the tree. She found her doll right on top of the pile, guarding it.

"Doll," whispered Priya. "Should we take the gold home and try to find its owner?"

"Yes dear, do," said the doll, so Priya left with the doll and the gold. Safe at home, she locked the door and stared at the treasure. After a while, she heard a loud knock on the door.

"Who is it?" she asked fearfully.

The knock was repeated, even louder.

"If I don't open, they may break the door," she thought. "I'll take a peek and scream if it's the robbers." With trembling fingers, she slid back the bolt and opened the door just a little. And there she saw . . . her husband. Happily she cried, "How good to see you! I thought you were the robbers come for the gold."

"What!" shouted Hari. "What gold, what robbers? Did you start to steal while I was away? I can't stay with a thief." Much upset, he turned to go but Priya pulled him inside.

"Wait, husband, and listen," she said, and told him of her night's adventure.

"Priya, forgive me," said her husband. "You saved the gold that I earned. Last night three robbers stole this gold from me as I returned home through the woods. Here, thank you." And he pushed the gold toward her.

"But husband, you earned it," she said, pushing it toward him.

"You saved it," he replied and pushed it back. Several times the gold went back and forth until finally Priya cried out, "Wait, wait, we will share this, of course." And she picked up her doll.

"Doll," she said. "I don't think that I will need you any more for my questions. I really do know the answers myself. But I still want you as a friend. I will put you on the shelf and surround you often with fresh flowers. Before that, though, one last question. "Should we share the gold and live happily ever after?"

And the doll said, "Yes dear, do." So they did!

The Loyal Parrot

Friendship in South India is built on loyalty and continues over time. Many well-known tales from the *Panchatantra* and other Indian story collections illustrate the importance of friendship through animal characters such as this kind bird.

Once in a peaceful forest, a hunter walked, holding arrows with poisoned tips. He heard a sound, saw a deer leap out, and immediately let loose an arrow. The arrow flew by the deer and hit instead a large, lovely tree. Annoyed at his miss, the hunter left the forest, never to return.

But the arrow's poison stayed in the tree, spreading quickly through it. Little by little, the tree started to die. In days, its leaves drooped sadly. Many of the creatures that lived in it moved away, fearing death. More leaves fell, and soon nothing was left on the wounded tree except for one small parrot. This parrot stayed, perched on a tree branch, even though there was no food to eat and no leaves to shelter him.

One day Indra, the king of Heaven, saw a bright light surrounding a tree on the Earth below. Curious, he went down and found a glow coming from a small parrot, who looked very weak and thin.

"Dear bird," said Indra. "This tree is almost dead; it can no longer help you. Why do you stay on it? You may die if you don't seek other shelter and food."

"My lord," said the parrot. "I was born in this tree. I ate my first food here. The tree has been my friend for a long time, giving me both shelter and company. Now that he is weak and hurt, how can I leave? He helped me as I grew. I must now stay and comfort my friend."

Indra, impressed by the parrot's words and spirit, said gently, "Little bird, you know much about true friendship and giving. I would like to grant you a blessing. What do you wish?"

"Great Indra," replied the bird, "all that I ask is for my friend, the tree, to be brought back to full health once again."

As soon as the words fell from the parrot's beak, the tree began to recover. Brown leaves suddenly turned green, bark began to glisten, bent branches straightened proudly. And the happy parrot nestled closer to the tree, as if to say, "Welcome back, dear friend."

A Guest Is Always Welcome

South Indian hospitality falls upon one like welcome monsoon rains. There seems, at times, no limit to how much can be given, as in this little tale.

Long ago, in the land of the Tamils, there lived a family well known for its hospitality. No one was turned away from their home, no one ever given too little. And so it was that one evening, a holy man stood at their door. At once, with a smile, a woman invited him in. She begged him to sit, then graciously gave him cool water. As he rested upon a mat, she cooked a meal for him then called to her son.

"Go now and find the best banana leaf to hold our guest's rice," she said. "Hurry so we don't keep him waiting."

The young boy ran eagerly outside and chose a large banana leaf for a plate. But as he picked it up, a sharp pain suddenly flowed through him. Pulling his hand back in surprise, he saw a poisonous snake drop to the ground and slither away. With his body on fire from the poison, the boy still remembered his guest. Clutching the leaf, he stumbled back to the kitchen. He handed it to his mother, his lips now dark from the poison. Then he fell upon the floor, his life taken by the snake.

Seeing the bite marks upon the boy's hand, the mother understood. He was her eldest son, very dear to her heart, and he was dead. With a grief beyond words, she called her husband.

"See what terrible thing has happened to our son," she said to him. "My own heart is torn from me and lies on the ground there. I cannot bear the pain. Yet we have a guest and cannot upset him now. What shall we do?"

The husband looked at the too-quiet boy he so loved and sorrow overcame him. After a moment he said gently, "We cannot help our child any more, so let us serve our guest, being careful that he learns nothing of our pain." Then he tenderly carried the boy's body into the corner and placed a cloth over it.

With their faces most controlled, the couple now served their guest. The wife laid down the leaf gathered by her son and placed upon it a mound of rice, mango pickle, thick sambar soup.

"I thank you for your kindness," said the wise guest. "Now call your family, so that I may bless them."

The other children came running, and as the parents apologized for the absence of their eldest, they suddenly heard a familiar and beloved voice.

As if returning from the yard, his eyes bright with the pleasure of serving a guest, their son ran through the door, healed by that special guest. Can you imagine his parents' joy? The family sat together and shared the happiest meal of their lives, while their guest sat calmly, well satisfied.

Krishna and Sudama

This familiar tale of friendship and divine help features Krishna, one of the incarnations of Lord Vishnu.

Krishna and Sudama studied and played together in the forest ashram of Guru Sandipani. When their schooling was finished they parted, pledging to meet again. Krishna became a king, and Sudama lived as a poor priest with a large family.

Much of Sudama's time was spent in meditation, while his wife, Sushila, tried desperately to stretch their few coins. Again and again, she went to the neighbors to borrow a bit of rice, until at last they would give her no more. She was a kind and patient woman, but her heart ached when she saw how weary her husband looked, how little her children had.

"My husband," she said at last. "We are starving. I do not mind if I go hungry, but I cannot bear to see our children so weak. Perhaps you could visit your old friend Krishna. He would surely help us a little."

Her husband was troubled but tempted. He did not want to beg for help from a friend, yet he did long to see Krishna.

"All right, I shall go," agreed Sudama. "I would love to see him again. But I will not talk about our trouble, and I must bring a gift."

"You told me that Krishna always liked that flattened rice," said Sushila. "I will try to get some."

She managed to borrow a little rice from her only friend and wrapped it carefully in a scrap of old cloth. Clutching his gift, Sudama set off. As he came at last to Krishna's palace, Krishna ran out with open arms and eagerly brought his tired guest inside.

When Krishna saw how weak his friend looked, he and his wife, Rukmini, gave him special care. Krishna himself washed Sudama's feet while Rukmini rubbed soothing sandalwood paste on his legs. They fanned him gently with a peacock feather fan.

Sudama enjoyed a fine meal and a night of great comfort. He talked joyfully with his friend, remembering their happy times together as students. Yet seeing the riches all around, Sudama felt shy about his gift. Krishna knew this and spoke to him gently.

"Do you not know that anything, no matter how small, if offered with love and devotion, is dear to me?" he said. "And a gift, no matter how grand, if offered without such love and faith, is worthless." Reassured, Sudama gave Krishna the rice.

"My favorite food," said Krishna, truly pleased. Sudama felt very happy as he watched Krishna eat a handful. And at that moment, something special happened. Krishna was about to eat some more rice when his wife stopped him. "Another handful, my lord, would be too much. One will give more than enough for a lifetime."

Sudama did not understand her words, but felt glad that Krishna enjoyed the gift. Then suddenly he thought of his poor wife and wished to return home. With love, Krishna said good-bye to his friend then watched him walk away.

Sudama journeyed on, content with his visit, pleased that he had not begged. "I did not ask him for anything, but he gave so freely of his love. What a dear friend he is," thought the priest.

As he neared his home, he began to worry about his family. But when he approached his old hut, he could not find it. In its place stood a grand house.

"What has happened?" he thought. "Has my family been killed and a rich neighbor come to stay?"

Suddenly a woman glowing like a goddess approached him, her silver ankle bells jingling. Boys and girls in fine silks walked with her. He was puzzled until he recognized his wife and children.

"Thank you for seeking Krishna's help," she said.

"But I didn't ask him for anything," said Sudama in confusion.

"Well, he knew of our problems," said Sushila. "He is your great friend and he must have known from your face. Soon after you left, our old house fell down. Suddenly, this one came up in its place, filled with fine foods, clothes, and gold coins in piles. We will never starve again."

Sudama shook his head and closed his eyes in thanks to his dear friend. He understood now why Rukmini stopped Krishna from eating more rice. All of this new wealth, more than enough for the rest of his life, had come when Lord Krishna swallowed just one handful of his gift.

Humbled and thankful, the family lived in the mansion, surrounded but not ruled by riches. For even as their thoughts had been fixed on prayer when poor, they lived still with great faith, sharing their wealth with others and worshipping daily.

Chapter 7

Hard Work and Study

In South India, education is very important. The students and parents are serious about learning. The students have respect for teachers. It is said that teaching helps the giver as well as the one who receives.

Lakshmi Sanga, Seattle

Adi male, adi pattal Ammiyum nagarum. Hit again and again, even the heavy grinding stone will move.

Tamil proverb

For thousands of years, people have studied and worked hard in South India. Students were taught in temples, in private homes, or as they learned a trade. Farmers, artisans, and many others worked long hours before and after the British turned India into a colony. Huge irrigation tanks and systems created earlier for South India's most common work—agriculture—impressed one British expert who estimated in 1850 that there were 50,000 such tanks in Madras Presidency (Tamil Nadu and neighboring areas). He observed that "The extent to which irrigation has been carried throughout is truly extraordinary. A moderate estimate of length of one embankment is 1/2 mile; thus there are in all almost 30,000 miles of embankments, sufficient to put a belt around the globe not less than six feet thick" (Alvares 1986, 14).

In the stories here, hard work and study are admired, while the tendency to lazily dream is discouraged.

A butterfly rests in a kolam.

A Pot of Dreams

Once in India, there was a girl who

loved to dream and scheme,

yet didn't like to work.

One day, her mother sent her to the market, although the
girl complained bitterly.

She carried a clay pot full of buttermilk to sell,

and since it was hot and she was lazy, she stopped often to rest.

During one stop, under a shady banyan tree,

she stared at the buttermilk and drifted into a dream, planning her
future.

"When I sell that buttermilk, I'll buy some eggs," she thought.

"The eggs will hatch, then I'll have chickens.

So I'll sell the chickens and buy a goat!

Then I'll sell the goat and buy a bull."

She smiled lazily and kept on dreaming.

"When I sell the bull, I'll buy trees—mango, papaya, and
coconut trees.

Later, I'll sell their fruits and buy a field!"

She pictured a green field ready for rice and grinned.

"I'll plant the field, then I'll have piles of rice.

I'll sell the rice, then build a fine house.

While I rest on its porch, some flies might come.

But if the flies bother me,

I'll kick them like this."

The girl kicked her leg at make-believe flies.

But her leg hit the pot.

The buttermilk spilled all over, making rivers for ants.

All the girl's grand plans and dreams disappeared, just like the buttermilk.

Only the hot sun remained.

Empty-handed, she returned home and her mother began to scold.

"Wait," said the girl. "Think how lucky we are.

What if I had taken our old cow?

When I kicked her, she would have run far away.

Today we lost a little buttermilk, but we still have our cow."

With her clever words, she calmed her mother down.

But after that day, the girl seemed a different child.

She worked all the time to make her dreams come true.

Whenever she went to the market, she never stopped to rest.

But she never again took buttermilk to sell.

Instead, she always carried hard, hard coconuts.

King's Questions

Once, long ago, two men started to work for a king at the same pay, doing the same job—cleaning the royal stables. Ten years later, one of them had become the king's closest advisor, while the other was still cleaning the stables. The stablehand grew jealous of the advisor, wondering why he had done so well. Finally he could hide his curiosity no longer. He went before the king and bowed.

"Your majesty," he said. "If it please you, do tell me why I am still a stablehand while another who started work with me is now your trusted advisor."

As the king was about to answer, they heard the sounds of a cart's bells outside. "Go see who is making that sound!" ordered the king. The man rushed out and came back shortly, saying, "A newly married couple, sir."

"From where do they come?" asked the king. The man rushed outside again and then reported, "They live in Mysore, sir."

"And why are they traveling?" the king inquired. A bit tired, the man ran out again. In moments he returned and said, "They went to visit some relative, your highness."

"What type of work do they do?" the king then asked. Hoping that this would be the final question, the man stopped the couple once again. Soon he came back to report, "They are merchants, sir."

Just then, the king's advisor entered the palace room. The king turned to him and said, "Outside, I hear the bells of a cart. Go see who is making that sound." With a bow, the advisor left and was back in a moment.

"Your majesty," he said. "There are two people, newly married. They live in Mysore, but the woman's father is not well, so they went to visit him in Vellore. They are merchants who sell bangles in their small shop near a Siva temple."

At that, the king turned to the stablehand. "Now, do you understand why you still work with the horses and he tells me how to rule the land? He found out more in one trip than you did in four!"

Mouse Merchant

Once in Andhra land, a mother sent her son to a nearby city to seek his fortune. As he stood there in confusion, he overheard a noble-looking man talking with a friend.

"Dear friend," said the first. "You have gained so much wealth. What is your secret?"

"Hard work and enterprise," replied the rich man. Then he pointed to a dead mouse in the street. "Look at that mouse. A clever person willing to work could make a fortune even from that."

The two walked on, laughing, as the young man stared at the tiny body. "How can I make money from that?" he wondered. "Well, let me try." He picked it up by the tail and started to walk, wondering what to do with a dead mouse.

No ideas came to him, so he was about to throw it away when a hungry-looking cat came bounding up.

"Here, boy," said the cat's owner. "May I buy that mouse for my cat?"

The young man nodded, gave it to the cat, and accepted one copper coin. His grin almost reached his ears.

"My first earnings," he thought with delight. "Now what shall I do with this one little coin?" He thought and thought, trying to find something small he could buy and sell. Just then he remembered the fields he had passed on his travels and had an idea. He ran to the market and bought a little palm sugar and a small clay pot. At a well, he filled the pot with water, then carried water and sugar to the outskirts of the city.

At twilight, those who picked flowers for a living began to return with weary steps. Thirsty from the hot sun, they dragged their feet. As they approached the city gate, the young man stepped forward and politely said, "You must be tired. Please have a sip of water and a bit of sugar to give you strength." Eagerly the workers did as he suggested and, in return for his kindness, they each gave him a small bunch of flowers.

"Ah," he said, satisfied. "Now I have earned many flowers. What shall I do with them?" The sound of a temple bell helped him decide. He ran to a big temple and stood outside, selling his flowers as offerings for the gods. When all the flowers were sold, he had several coins. Early the next morning, he bought more sugar. Again he offered water and sugar to the workers and received more flowers to sell. The next day, he bought even more sugar and a bigger pot. After weeks of serving the flower sellers, he went as well to the fields where workers cut hay. They were delighted to share his refreshment. "We can give you nothing now," they said. "But when you need our hay, it is yours."

Soon after that, a great storm came, sending twigs and branches falling all round.

"If I got money from a dead mouse," thought the young man, "I can also get money from dead wood." He ran around the city, picking up and selling the wood he found. With the money he had earned, he bought a stall where he could both sleep and sell more wood. As his sales increased, he one day heard good news. A merchant would soon pass by with horses to sell to a neighboring king. He would need hay for the horses.

Quickly, the young man found his friends in the field and said, "I would now like what you promised me. And I want your word that you will sell hay to no one else tomorrow." Everyone agreed to bring hay to the young man's place alone.

At noon, when the horse dealer rode through the city, he was puzzled to find no one selling hay. He started to ride out to the fields but stopped when he saw the young man's stall, with bundles stacked high beside it.

"Hello," he called, and the young man ran out. "Will you sell this hay to me, my son? I will pay you well." Of course the young man agreed and loaded the bundles on the merchant's cart. In return, he was given a bag of gold coins.

With that money, he built a big shop and a fine house. His fortunes continued to improve, and he brought his mother to share his wealth. Then he made a golden mouse and gave it to the man who had first inspired him.

"Why do you give me this?" asked the older merchant. "I have never seen you before."

"My fortune began after hearing your wise words, sir," said the young man, and he told the story of his climb to wealth. Much impressed, the merchant asked his clever daughter to marry the young man. She agreed, the two were married, and half of the family's fortune was given to the couple.

When he moved into his new home, the young man made careful arrangements for the flower and hay cutters to receive water and sugar daily. After that, he and his wife worked well together so that both their fortune and their love grew and grew. Thus, they lived a rich, happy life. And just think, it all started with one dead mouse!

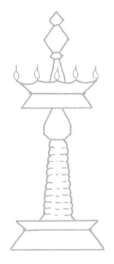

The Guru

Once in the eighteenth century, in what is now Kerala, a young boy, named Mani, wanted to be a fighter. When he was old enough he went to a nearby city seeking a teacher.

Fortunately, a prince there liked the boy and accepted him as a student. The prince was himself an expert in kalaripayattu, and the boy worked very hard with him. After one year of training, the prince asked the boy, "How many people can you now fight at one time?"

"One thousand men," said the boy proudly. But his teacher was not pleased. The boy's studies continued for another year. He had his limbs massaged with oil to make them supple, and he learned how to move his body like an acrobat's. At the end of the second year, the teacher asked, "Now how many people could you fight at once?"

"At least five hundred men," said the boy with a grin. Again, the teacher seemed disappointed. Studies went on as Mani learned to stretch his legs, to balance, to leap high. A year passed quickly and the question came once more.

"I could hold off one hundred men," bragged the boy. Shaking his head, the teacher said nothing but continued teaching. The boy learned to use weapons of wood, large and small. After that year, the question came, and Mani said "fifty." Several more years passed, as he learned to use swords, spears, and deadly knives. And each time the question was asked, his answer was lower.

At last, after long years of study, the teacher asked, "Today how many men could you successfully hold off?"

"Sir, I honestly feel now that I could resist one man," replied Mani in a low voice. Finally the teacher smiled, pleased with the boy's answer. For Mani had worked hard enough and well enough to learn the most important lesson of a fighter and leader: humility.

Soon after that, Mani went to take an oil bath, when suddenly two men with great swords leapt out at him. At once he spun round, ready to fight. But then he heard a loud clap and looked over to see his teacher.

"Congratulations, my boy," said the teacher proudly. "You have proved that you can think quickly, as a fighter must. I asked those men to test you and you showed skill and courage. You have indeed learned all that I know. Go now and help those who need you."

Sadly, Mani left his guru and began to teach a young prince in southern Kerala. As a guru, Mani received much fame and honor, and his student worked hard. The young prince, too, was asked the question over and over, and his answers grew steadily more humble the more he studied. Finally, he too said simply, "I could perhaps hold off one man." His guru smiled, well satisfied, for his pupil had at last proved himself worthy. The boy continued to study and grew up to be Rama Varma, a famous warrior and ruler. And even when surrounded by silks and gold, he still worked hard, never forgetting his wise guru.

The Squirrel's Stripes

Rama's march to the island of Lanka is an exciting episode in the famous *Ramayana*. When his army of monkeys and bears reaches the sea, they need to build a bridge to Lanka. Everyone works very hard to help, even a little squirrel.

As the great construction began, Rama suddenly noticed a small squirrel. Sitting on his little feet, the squirrel watched as stones and sand were dropped into the water to make a bridge. All at once, he fell down on his back and rubbed it in the sand. Then, running on short but eager feet, the squirrel raced to the bridge, dodging the bigger animals who were working steadily.

He hopped up on the bridge and searched for cracks between the big stones. When he saw a spot where sand was needed, he shook, shook, shook his back with all his might. Sand sprinkled through the air right into the crack.

Satisfied, the squirrel returned to the beach. He fell down once more, rubbed more sand on his back, then scurried to the bridge. There, again, he shook off the sand to fill another crack. Over and over this small animal worked, all on his own, with no one but Rama even noticing him. At last, he was exhausted and stopped near Rama for a moment.

"Little one, you worked so hard. Please rest," said Rama gently. As he spoke, he stroked the squirrel's back. His fingers in the soft fur made three little lines. Ever since then, many squirrels in India have three stripes running down their backs, as a reward for that squirrel's great effort. And still today those marks remind us that the hard work of even one so little can help so much.

Chapter 8

Heroes and Inspiration

Indians respect the man of learning, the hero, the man of wisdom, and the holy man much more than the man who has money. This has been true for thousands of years, and it is still true today.
(Dhar 1973, 23)

Powerful is not he who knocks the other down. Indeed powerful is he who controls himself when he is angry.
Sayings of Prophet Muhammad

In South India there are many heroes: wise saints, just rulers, freedom fighters who resisted the British, those who fought the wrongs of caste. One popular Muslim *pir* (holy man), Hazarat Shams Paran, wrote fine poetry and had such power that "even in his old age he could beat a wrestler by means of his inward strength and make him roll along like a stone from the hilltop" (Bayly 1989, 112).

The tales of heroes are passed on through song and story and engraved as well on stone markers. Thousands of these hero stones are found in South India, especially in Tamil Nadu and Karnataka. They praise those

who died fighting in battles, protecting their villages, or hunting fierce animals. Some hero stones honor women who sacrificed themselves, saints who underwent great hardships, and even courageous animals. South India has many heroes indeed; here are just a few.

The lotus, a symbol of purity and beauty.

The Elephant King

The theme of sacrifice runs through South Indian life, thus many heroes serve as examples of such nobility. "The Elephant King" is a Buddhist *Jataka* tale, one of the 550 stories telling of the Buddha's many lifetimes on Earth. In a number of them, the Buddha sacrifices himself in some form: as a monkey king, a parrot, a prince, an elephant king. . . .

Once in India, in a valley ringed by mountains, there lived a kind elephant king with skin of shining white and tusks that glowed like gold. He ruled more than eight thousand elephants in a peaceful land of lotus blooms and water lilies. The king had two wives, and he loved them both the same, but for some reason his second wife grew jealous. Every day, she looked round with envious eyes, always finding something to make those feelings grow. One day, for instance, the king was walking with his queens in the forest when he saw a lovely tree bright with blossoms.

"Stand under this, my queens, and I shall decorate your backs," he said. As the two elephants stood under the tree, the king wrapped his trunk round it and shook it. Flowers fluttered down upon the first queen, but upon the second, no flowers fell, only dead worms. And thus her jealousy grew.

Several days later, the king went with his queens to bathe in a cool river. A servant from a far land came, bearing a brilliant white lotus. He offered it to the king to honor him.

"I have no need of this," said the king and gave it to the queen standing nearby. She was, of course, the first queen. Thus, the second queen's jealousy grew and grew until she wished only for the king's death.

Yet she knew that alone she could never kill him, surrounded as he was by hundreds of servants and guards. She pondered the problem until one day a solution appeared in the form of three holy men. These wandering sages came hungry to her land, and the queen served them well with sweet water, soft berries, and fine nuts. Then she sang to them a gentle song. They were well pleased and asked to repay her kindness.

"Well, dear friends," she said sweetly. "If you could help me, I do have one small request. You see, I am very tired of living in this body. Could you make me die and then come back to Earth as a human princess?"

Such a wish was easily granted. In a few days the queen died. Months later she was born as a human princess. She grew in the best of palaces, eating the finest foods, sleeping always on silk. Yet inside her heart she had only one thought still, one carried from her last life—the elephant king must die!

Finally, when she became a queen, she started the next part of her plan. She stretched out upon the royal bed, pretending to be deathly ill. Her husband, the king, was greatly worried.

"My dearest wife," he cried. "What can I do to help? What medicine can I bring?"

"There is only one thing that could help me now," she whispered. "Far from here is a valley of elephants. The king of these beasts is a creature with shining tusks. If by some means you could have him killed and his tusks brought to me, I need only to rub them and I will be cured."

"It shall be done," promised the king, and his royal drums sounded, calling all the hunters in the kingdom. Soon, a line of proud hunters stretched out near the palace like a long turban. The king walked back and forth seeking the strongest of the strong, the best of all the rest. At last he chose the greatest hunter and brought him to the queen. She pointed to far-off mountains and asked, "Can you really cross all of those to find and kill the elephant king?"

"I love killing elephants," he roared. "I shall cut off his head, make his shoulders best friends, and bring you the tusks."

"If you do, I will make you so wealthy you need never work again," she promised.

The greedy eyes of the hunter glowed as he bowed and left. He made himself strong sandals, leather rope, and the sharpest of arrows. Then he began to walk. Over mountains, through valleys, sleeping on stones, feasting on ferns, he walked for seven years, seven months,

The Elephant King

and seven days. At last, he came to the kingdom of the elephants. He saw one, two, ten, one hundred, eight thousand elephants. And he grew worried.

"How can I kill the king by myself?" he wondered. "He is always surrounded by others."

But the hunter soon noticed that at times the elephant king went alone to bathe in the river. "That is when I shall kill him," decided the hunter. He dug a deep hole near the river and crouched in it, waiting.

Finally, one very hot afternoon, his wait was over. The elephant king came slowly, making great elephant yawns, looking weary indeed.

"Today is the day," thought the hunter. "He is weak and tired." Immediately, he let loose his poisoned arrows. But although they hit the elephant, they did not kill him. Instead, bright red dripped down his white skin and he stood still. The hunter was afraid now, for a wounded elephant is truly dangerous. Slowly, he crept forward and soon was so close that the elephant could have stomped upon him, crushed him, or thrown him up with strong tusks. Yet the elephant only turned gentle eyes upon the hunter and said, "Come, you wish my tusks. You may cut them off. I shall not harm you."

So the hunter began to chip away at the tusks. But he too was tired, with his knife no longer sharp and the tusks so very thick. After several painful hours, the elephant again spoke, his face covered with blood, his eyes still kind but now wet with pain.

"You cannot do it; you are too weak. Come, let me help you before my strength is gone. Put the knife in my trunk." The hunter did as he was told and the elephant held the knife, making it fall again and again on his tusks, on his own body. At last the tusks fell down in a pool of red blood, and the elephant sank upon the earth, released from this world.

The hunter slowly picked up the tusks and wiped them. Then, by the magic of the tusks, he returned to the palace in seven days. He rushed to the queen and thrust them into her hands.

"Here, take them," he cried. "And don't reward me. Why did you have me kill such a kind being? He never hurt you nor anyone. He helped me even as I tried to harm him. Why did you want this? Why?" Then that brave hunter fled from the palace, tears still in his eyes. And they say from that day on, he never again harmed a living creature.

As for the queen, she held the elephant's tusks in her hands at last. She had waited for so long and now he was dead. Yet instead of feeling great joy and triumph, she suddenly felt shame and sorrow. She locked the tusks in a chest, then her heart weakened, and she fell lifeless to the floor.

But the story does not end there. For the queen came back many lifetimes upon this Earth in various forms, and the elephant king as well, as a potter, a royal elephant, a prince. Then one night, the two again shared part of a lifetime. She was now a nun who went in the evening to hear a wise teacher preach and tell stories. And this teacher was none other than the kind elephant king, come back now as the great Lord Buddha.

The Elephant King

King Kumanan

Kings of old were revered for their valor in battle, their generosity, faith, and justice. King Kumanan, mentioned in the work of the Tamil poets in the Sangam era, is a fine example of such a king. In one poem, a hungry poet, Peruncittiranaar, vows to ask Kumanan for help because he is known for giving "like a rain cloud that pours with thunder and lightning on wide fields scorched and plowed by hunters" (Ramanujan 1985, 134).

Hear now of Kumanan,
born in a clan without stain,
famed for its victories.

King of the Tamil people, Kumanan ruled with such goodness that the tiger sat with the deer, and hunger fled from the land. Poets came from afar to sound his praise, and when he heard a pleasing line, his delight poured forth with gifts of gold. Now in this kingdom where happiness walked, there was one man with a jealous heart—the king's own brother, Hammonan. For he wanted to be king, to have great wealth and power all for himself. And so he began to plot the king's death.

Word of his plan soon reached the ears of King Kumanan, yet he was not angry. Instead he called at once for his brother.

"Dear brother," he said. "I have heard that you wish to be king and would kill me to have the crown. Please take this throne. I want no bloodshed or struggle. I shall go willingly to the woods." He stepped down from the throne, then simply walked out of the palace and towards the quiet forest.

Hammonan eagerly took over and ruled with cruelty—taxing the people unfairly and ignoring their needs while spending his time in idle pleasures. Outside the palace, the earth mourned, the rains stopped, and the cows bellowed in distress. He was hated and feared by all.

Meanwhile, under kind banyan trees, Kumanan lived peacefully. He bathed among bamboos, lit fires of wood brought by wild elephants, and plucked leaves for food. After some time, the wise men and poets who had adorned his court found their way to the forest. There, they sang for him once again and offered poems. In the woods he had no gold, so he gladly gave them forest fruits and flower garlands.

Hammonan soon grew worried when he heard of all who flocked to Kumanan. "He may be planning to overthrow me," thought Hammonan. "And even if he isn't, he will become a threat to me in the future as his followers grow. I will not rest until he is dead."

Hammonan then offered a reward of ten thousand gold coins for his brother's head. Yet no one wanted the reward, for everyone still loved noble Kumanan. Months passed. One day a poor poet wandered through the woods, seeking Kumanan. At last he stood before the former king and played his harp, singing of his wife who cooked greens from the garbage. Kumanan wished to help the man who had so little, to give him more than just flowers. Yet he had nothing else and so grew sad until he remembered the reward for his head.

"Come, my friend," he said happily. "Take this to the king right now. He will pay you well." Then he picked up a large knife and held it, about to cut his own throat.

"NO, NO, STOP!" cried the poet and those near Kumanan. They rushed to his side, pulling the knife out of his hands.

"Sir," said the poet. "I could never take your life. But I will take your idea and bring the head your brother so desires. Thank you." He returned to his home, found the softest of wood, and sculpted it into the rough shape of a head. Covering the head with a cloth, he sprinkled goat's blood upon it and ran to the palace.

"I have your brother's head, as you wished, sir," he cried to the king. "Now reward me well." As the poet thrust the plate forward, Hammonan smelled the scent of death and saw fresh blood. Under the cloth he saw the shape of a nose, the outline of a face. Suddenly he fainted. When at last he regained consciousness, he seemed a different man.

"Why did I have my own brother killed?" he moaned. "What horrible crime have I done? I must take my own life now." Feeling great sadness and guilt, he was about to strike himself when the poet stepped forward again.

"Stop, sir, and hear my news of joy," he said. "Look carefully once more at this head." He pulled the cloth off of the head. The king stopped his tears, stared at the head, then slowly started to laugh. Others soon joined in, greatly relieved. The poet was well rewarded, and so was the kingdom. For Hammonan now knew who should rule and made arrangements to bring back his brother.

Days later, as the sun smiled, Hammonan led a long, happy parade of his subjects into the forest, seeking their king. He bowed before his brother, begging him to rule again. Kumanan agreed at last and ruled for many years in peace, with his brother as his closest and best advisor. Under their just rule, the sun shared its strength, the rains fell as they should, and the land blossomed once more.

The Bell of Justice

One sign of a good ruler is a willingness to right wrongs and provide justice for all. Often this was done long ago when a king or a trusted advisor went in disguise around the kingdom, rooting out any problems found. At other times, a bell or signal was to be sounded when injustice had occurred.

Once in the land of Telugu speakers, a king was known for his just rule. By day and night, people felt safe in their homes or in the streets. Yet still the king searched daily for ways to improve the kingdom, to make the people more content.

One morning, he had a large bell placed in the center of the city, then sent out a royal decree:

> "Let any and all who have a problem or who have suffered injustice, ring this bell at once. It is the king's promise that any wrong will then be righted so that all, great and small, can live without worry."

The bell was often silent, for there were few complaints in the land. Yet when it rang, the king himself came to hear the problem and quickly sent soldiers to have justice done. Thus the citizens lived happily, praising the king.

Now in this kingdom lived an old soldier and his old horse. Although the horse had been the soldier's companion for many years, he now found the effort of feeding the horse to be a trouble. "After all," thought the soldier, "she is only a horse. Let her find food for herself." Soon the soldier let her go, and she wandered sadly through the city, seeking a little grass to eat.

One day the horse was nibbling some weeds near the bell when a merchant walked past and suddenly stopped. "The bell's rope looks very weak, I must go tell the palace guards," he thought. "But the rope might fall off before it can be replaced. I'll put something up for now."

He looked around and found some strong vine growing nearby. Quickly he pulled out a long piece, attached it to the bell, then walked away, planning to tell the guards the next day.

Just then, the hungry horse looked up. When she saw the inviting green vine, she started at once to eat and eat. As she chewed, she pulled the bell back and forth, back and forth, causing a loud, steady ring. Hearing the bell, the king sent his soldiers to find out the problem. They soon saw the horse.

"What a clever horse," they said. "Now what could be her problem?"

"She looks quite weak," said one guard. "Let us find her owner and inquire about her health." After questioning a number of people, they found the soldier. They soon heard of his neglect, so he was brought to the king's court.

"This poor animal deserves justice too," said the king. "No one shall be refused help in my kingdom. She served you for many years, so you must care for her now. From this day on, you must give her what is fair and see that she never goes in want."

The soldier left, feeling most guilty, and led his horse home. Thus, until the horse died a gentle death of old age, the soldier took good care of her. He shared what he had with a willing heart, pleased to live in a land where even animals could find justice.

Avvaiyar's Rest

Avvaiyar lived almost 2,000 years ago in Tamil Nadu. She is one of the many wise sages and saints of South India. Avvaiyar is remembered as an elder poet who wandered the land, teaching people through songs and poems that are still shared in schools and homes today.

One evening Avvaiyar walked slowly past coconut palms while cows returned home for the night. The bells on their horns sang out as the light softened, threaded with red. Tired now, she searched for a place to rest and was pleased to find a temple.

Avvaiyar sat down, leaned back against a tree, and stretched her weary legs out. They pointed right toward the statue of a god.

Suddenly a young man, the temple priest, came running up to her. "Old woman," he cried. "Don't you see what you are doing? You are insulting the god by pointing your feet right toward him. Move them at once."

"My son," she said with a sigh. "I will be delighted to move them away from the god. Simply tell me in which direction there is no god, and there will I point my feet."

Obavva of the Pestle

South Indian folk ballads are rich in tales of local people who became local heroes, many of them for simple acts: skill in sports,
winning competitions for lifting heavy stones, even setting records
for weeding or cutting wood. Obavva is one such hero who became
widely known in Karnataka. She was an ordinary woman who used
an ordinary stone pestle (for grinding rice) to do something very,
very brave.

Hundreds of years ago, India was divided into many kingdoms.
And in the kingdom of Chitradurga, King Nayaka ruled from a strong
fort, defending himself well. Hyder Ali, the king of Mysore, looked often at this kingdom, wishing to conquer it. But the fort was so well
made and well protected that he had great trouble.

One day he tried a new plan. He sent a soldier to befriend an enemy guard, hoping to learn the fort's secrets. The soldier returned
with valuable knowledge, telling Hyder Ali where a weak spot, a small
crack, could be found.

Hyder Ali and his troops set off. As they silently crawled up closer
to the spot, a guard stood on the inside wall near the crack. Every day
the guard watched this section, but it was now time to eat. Everything
seemed quiet enough, so he walked to his nearby home. His wife,
Obavva, served him, and, as he ate, he asked her for water.

"There is none here. I shall fetch it quickly," she said. Taking a
pot, she hurried down to the pond. Now, the crack was next to this
pond, so suddenly she heard sounds and whispers close to her. She
stood very still and listened. Then she saw a large stick scraping away
pieces of the wall. Thinking quickly, she picked up a heavy pestle
nearby and she stood right next to the hole.

Without moving, she watched as a soldier's head suddenly
emerged. She waited until the soldier was just about out of the wall;
then she hit him hard on the head, killing him. Immediately, she pulled
his body through the hole and pushed it to the side.

Outside the wall, they thought that the first soldier had entered, so the second one started in. Obavva waited again, holding her breath as a head, shoulders, then body appeared. When this one was almost inside, she hit him, killing him as well. Again, she pulled the body through and pushed it aside. The next soldier came and met the same fate, and the next. Bodies piled up next to this brave woman. But she grew tired, feeling the weight of the stone pestle.

When the next soldier came through, she hit him, but not hard enough. He was only wounded. He saw her and stumbled toward her. Another soldier followed and another. As she screamed a warning to those in the fort, the enemy soldiers closed around her, killing her. But her voice brought many who fought bravely. Thus, the enemy soldiers were captured, and the fort was saved. Ever since that day, the people of Chitradurga and the people of Karnataka love to tell the story of this simple, ordinary woman who became a true hero.

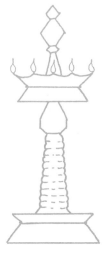

Resisting the British: Rani Channamma

Many South Indians of all backgrounds resisted the British. One of the most famous is the Muslim ruler from Mysore, Tippu Sultan, who fought fiercely against the British. He and his father, Hyder Ali, realized quickly how strong the British could become in India. Tippu struggled against them, often without Indian allies, until he was killed in battle in 1799. His oft-quoted words sum up his contempt for early Indian friends of the British: "Better to die like a soldier than to live as a miserable dependent on the infidels in the list of their pensioned rajas."

In Tamil Nadu, the ruler Kottabomman was another popular patriot. When an unfair tax was demanded from him, he resisted, saying his legendary words, "Not a dime from me for these foreign beggars."

Once his brother, while fleeing from the British, was helped by a clever old woman who hid him in her home. She covered him with a white cloth, sprinkled turmeric water on it, then hung neem leaves across the door. When the British soldiers came to search her home and saw these obvious warning signs of smallpox, they ran away instead! (Rajamanickam 1985)

Many in South India know of Rani Channamma (1756-1829), a queen of Kittur, Karnataka, who was one of the first to resist the British.

Brave from childhood, Rani Channamma met her husband in a fight over a dead tiger. One day, the ruler of Kittur went hunting a tiger that was frightening his subjects. Proud of his skill, he scented the animal in the forest, took aim, and shot. He followed the tiger's cry, but found one tiger with two arrows. Next to the animal stood a proud young woman who claimed that it was her arrow that killed the tiger, not his!

After the two stopped fighting, she soon became his queen and second wife. As an able leader, Rani Channamma helped to rule the kingdom. Then the king, tricked into meeting enemies in Pune, was held captive there for the rest of his life. During his absence, she managed the country well, and after his death, she ruled along with his frail son until he died in 1824.

At this point, the leadership was to pass to an adopted heir. But the British refused to accept the new ruler. They made plans to take over the kingdom, which was of strategic use to them. Rani Channamma tried to rally neighboring kingdoms to fight against the British. She urged her own people to resist the spreading tide of British rule in her stirring words:

"Kittur is ours. We are masters of our own territory. . . . These Britishers have come to our land on the pretext of carrying on trade, and now, seeing that we are quarreling amongst ourselves, they want to grab our land and rule over us. . . . But the people of Kittur love freedom more than life. Patriotism and the love of this sacred soil and freedom flows in their veins. Each one of us is equal to ten of their soldiers. Kittur will fight to the last. We would die rather than be slaves of the British."

Amazed to be resisted by a woman, the British brought cannons and soldiers to frighten Rani. But her forces captured several guns and soldiers. The British attacked her fort to free their men but were soundly defeated. Much humiliated, they soon gathered an overwhelming army, then demanded the release of several British officers in exchange for peace. The officers were returned to the British camp but the British broke their promise and attacked the fort. After two days of fierce battle, the large British force captured the fort. Rani Channamma, her head still held high, was imprisoned and died four years later in a cell. Ever since that time, her courage as one of the first to resist the British is still remembered in the ballads sung of her life and death.

Ramanujan

by Manu Samanna-Spagnoli

South India has also given the world heroes of science, like C. V. Raman, and heroes of mathematics, the most famous of whom was the brilliant Srinivasa Ramanujan. Ramanujan, who died at too young an age, is an inspiration to many around the world, a man whose work even today astounds and confounds mathematicians. Peter Borwein, of Dalhousie University, voiced what many mathematicians feel: "It's not possible to deal with Ramanujan's work without being awed by what he managed to accomplish" (Kanigel 1991, 267). His story is told in great detail in a biography by Kanigel, but here is an introduction to his life by Manu, age 10.

Ramanujan is important to me because he's from India and I'm half Indian. Also because he mastered a lot in math at a young age without many advantages. More than half of the results in his notebooks are new even now and not yet proved! Today's mathematicians are amazed at his discoveries and are still trying to work them out.

Ramanujan was born on December 22, 1887, in India. His family was quite poor. As a young child, he didn't talk much his first three years, then became a stubborn boy who asked many questions but hated sports. At 10, he scored first in exams in his district and entered Town High School. He was a good student in everything up until he discovered math. He knew math would be right for him when he mastered a college math book at the age of 12. After that, he only studied math and failed other subjects, so he had to leave college later on.

Ramanujan was poor and worked alone at his math. He kept a journal that he wrote in every day until he died. At first, other math people didn't listen to him when he asked for help. Then a British mathematician named G. H. Hardy decided to listen to him, and after reading Ramanujan's discoveries, he was really amazed. So in March 1914, Hardy got him a ticket to England, and Ramanujan and Hardy talked about math at Cambridge University for years. Living there, he started to get weak, mainly because he didn't eat meat. Most of the British food had meat in it, and he was used to leaving his vegetarian food up to Mom at home. So when he studied in England, he did not eat well, and finally he became very sick. He returned to India, still sick, and died at the age of 32.

Ramanujan made great discoveries in math. He published 37 papers and articles on math and left behind three notebooks with 3,000 theorems, without proofs. He always thought about math, even when he was sick, like in this true story:

One day, when Ramanujan was in the hospital, his friend Hardy came to visit. To cheer Ramanujan up, Hardy wanted to say something about math. So he said, "The taxi I came in had a very boring number, 1,729."

Ramanujan knew so much about numbers that he said, "No, that's not boring at all!"

GUESS WHY HE SAID THAT . . .

He told Hardy that 1,729 was a very interesting number "because 1,729 is the smallest number that can be written as the sum of the cubes of two numbers in two different ways."

$1^3 + 12^3 = 1729$ (1x1x1 + 12x12x12 = 1729)

and

$9^3 + 10^3 = 1729$ (9x9x9 + 10x10x10 = 1729) !!!!!!!!!!!

Chapter 9

Wit and Humor

To him who knows not to laugh, this infinite
universe would, in bright daylight,
seem plunged in darkness.
Tirukkural (Maharajan 1979, 25)

Nindu kunda tona kodu.
Empty vessels make the greatest sound.
Telugu proverb

People across South India enjoy jokes and humorous tales of all kinds, some familiar around the world, others more rooted in South India. Fool tales are common—about the farmer who burns his cotton to kill a bug, the thief who cooks a meal and wakes everyone, the boy who sits on a tree branch as he saws it off.

Stories of clever tricksters are much loved as well. In South India, the definite favorite is Tenali Raman, who chose "death by old age" when sentenced to die for one of his tricks. Modern jokes are told often; tellers of all ages enjoy poking fun at themselves, at outsiders, at politics, and at the world all round.

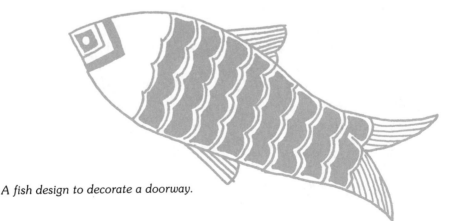

A fish design to decorate a doorway.

Tricksters and Tricks

Tenali Raman

Tenali Raman carried the name of his birthplace, the village of Tenali in Andhra Pradesh, into the court of the great Krishnadeva Raya, king of the Vijay-anagar Empire in sixteenth-century South India. Tenali Raman is known today through the many popular tales of his wit and of his ability to trick (and teach) even the king. In these three short tales, he helps those who need help, punishes those who cheat, and outwits the king.

A Queenly Yawn

Once Queen Tirumaladevi called Tenali Raman in.

"You must help me," she said.

"What is the problem?" asked Tenali Raman.

"I yawned," she replied.

"That is not so terrible, is it?"

"Well, the king thinks so," she answered sadly. "Three days ago, when he was reading his play to me, I suddenly had to yawn. He became furious and ordered me to leave. I'm afraid that I will never see him again."

"Your yawn may have discouraged him as a writer," said Tenali Raman. "But you meant no harm. I will try to help."

The next day, all of the king's ministers met to discuss ways of improving the rice harvest. Tenali Raman stepped up to the king, holding several rice grains in his hand.

"Your majesty," he said. "This rice will solve your problems and give everyone enough to eat. For each grain will produce three times more rice than a regular grain."

"How wonderful," said the king. "What is the secret? Does it need special soil? More water?"

"No, sir," replied Raman. "It only needs one thing."

"And what is that?" asked the king.

"It must be planted and harvested by someone who has never yawned."

"Never yawned?" said the king. "That's impossible. Everyone yawns at some time."

"Oh, of course you are right," said Tenali Raman. "Why didn't I remember that? Well, I'll go tell the queen what you said, for she may be interested."

"No, Raman," said the king with a sudden smile. "I understand my mistake. I will go now and speak to her myself." And he did.

Sweet Sorrow

Once the king received some sugar of excellent quality and ordered it spread out in the sun to dry. As it sat shining, Tenali Raman came to the court. The king, wanting the sugar all to himself, told Tenali Raman that it was special sand from the north and not to be touched. Tenali Raman listened to the king, looked at the sand, and walked home to think.

"Well, at last I have fooled Tenali Raman," said the king with great delight to his queen.

Some time later the queen looked outside. She spied Tenali Raman and his son throwing handfuls of the delicious sweetness into their mouths. When she told the king, he hurried out.

"What are you doing?" he roared.

"Your majesty," replied Tenali Raman, "we have just had terrible news. Our favorite cow has died, and to show our great sorrow, we are forcing ourselves to eat this terrible, dry sand."

With a laugh and a shake of his imperial head, the king let them go. But then he set several soldiers to guard what was left of the sugar.

Golden Mangoes

One day, Tenali Raman watched curiously as a line of priests filed out of the throne room. In their hands, each held a golden mango; on their faces, each had a smile.

"Why are the priests so well rewarded today?" Tenali Raman asked the king.

"They have just helped my mother's spirit," he replied. "Today is the anniversary of her death. I used to be sad since she died in the winter without fulfilling her last wish—to eat a summer mango. But the priests said that if I gave them each a golden mango, I could satisfy her wish. Now I know that my mother's spirit is content."

But Tenali Raman knew something else—that the greedy priests had cheated the king. He was angry and wanted to teach them a lesson.

"Thank you, your highness," he said. "You have given me an idea. My mother died two years ago, with an unfulfilled wish. I will do as you suggest and help her spirit, too." He bowed and left the king.

Word spread quickly through the palace about another wish to be satisfied. Thus, when an invitation came for dinner at Tenali Raman's home, the priests went happily, hoping for a fine gift.

"My friends," said Tenali Raman in greeting. "I have heard how you kindly helped the spirit of the king's mother. I beg you now to accept my mother's last wish, which awaits you in the courtyard."

"You are a good and wise son, Raman," said the chief priest, leading the others eagerly into the courtyard. As they stood waiting for a gift, Tenali Raman suddenly came toward them, carrying a heavy, iron rod.

"Before she died, my poor mother suffered from arthritis. Thus her last wish was to try a new cure for the disease—being hit hard with a heavy, iron rod. Thank you so much for fulfilling her wish," said Tenali Raman as he moved closer.

In a great hurry to flee, the priests ran into each other. Tenali Raman stood laughing while they raced out of his house and back to the palace. There, to avoid further trouble, they quickly returned their golden mangoes, begging the king's pardon.

When the king heard the full story, he laughed at the priests, then at himself, and finally rewarded Tenali Raman for teaching a well-deserved lesson to all.

A Real Bargain

In some Muslim areas of the south, a favorite trickster is Khwaja Nasruddin, known elsewhere by various names, including Abu Khan, Hodja, and Mullah. He plays many roles, sometimes a clever fool, sometimes a judge, sometimes a helpful friend.

One day Khwaja Nasruddin went to visit a friend who had just opened an inn. Above the door the owner had proudly written, "The Guest is Our Master." As the two talked, the very first customer came in and sat down. He was a large, rough man who bellowed to the owner, "Satisfy me or you'll be sorry." Then he held up a small coin, demanding, "With this money, I want to eat, drink, and be entertained."

The owner did not know what to do. He was afraid of the man's anger and truly wanted to please his first customer, but the request was impossible. A plate of rice alone would cost more than that little coin. He opened his mouth to apologize, when suddenly Khwaja Nasruddin took the coin, crossed the street, and bought something at the market there. He returned holding it happily in his hand.

"There you are. Enjoy yourself," he said with a bow. Then he gave the man a thin slice of watermelon. "Now you can eat the flesh, drink the juice, and spit the seeds for entertainment!"

The Fish Curry

Kerala is noted for its coconuts, its tender green mangoes, and its many temples to Kali (which often have large, open, pool-like tanks next to them), a fierce and powerful goddess. In some rituals there, Kali is said to possess certain people, then to speak and act through them. However, such possession can also be faked for other purposes, as in this trick by a clever wife.

Once, in lush Kerala, a farmer named Gopi sat down to rest near the cool tank of a Kali temple. As he gazed into the water, he saw the silver of fine fish. He was hungry, and they looked delicious.

It was forbidden to take anything from Kali, so he tried to ignore them. Instead he looked up. But there he saw fine green mangoes on a nearby tree. His stomach sang out, remembering how good fish curry with green mango could taste. Gopi shut his eyes to keep away temptation, but still he smelled fish curry cooking.

Suddenly he glanced around, then reached up, picked two mangoes and, rushing to the tank scooped up four fish. With his arms full of food, he hurried home and gave everything to his wife.

"Make a delicious fish curry," he said. "But don't tell anyone, because I took these from the Kali temple."

His wife, Kamala, started cooking while he went to plow. Soon, the smells of fish curry circled round the home, and she ran to call her husband. But he did not come.

"Perhaps before I call again, I should make sure the curry is good," she thought. So she took a very big taste. It was good. So good that she decided to have another taste. That was so good that she decided to eat her share right away. And she did. Then, trying to be fair, she called Gopi again to come eat. But he was working in a far field and didn't hear her, so she looked longingly at the curry.

"Well, since he isn't here, perhaps I should eat another serving before it becomes cold," she said to herself. So she ate some more and waited for him.

"Maybe he doesn't feel hungry now," she thought after she called him again. "I'll just have a little to help him." After she ate that, she said, "When he returns this will be too cold and then it is no good. I'll have a bit more so we don't waste it." She had some more and then a little more, and even more, until finally there was no curry left.

"Ah," she sighed. "Now I am in trouble. Why did I eat all of that? He will be furious. What can I do?" She thought and thought and then had a plan. It was well known in the village that when the goddess Kali was displeased, she could enter into a human to give her message. So Kamala filled the fish curry pot with mud, then tied a large leaf carefully around it. Next, she shook her hair loose, splashed water on her clothes, called her husband once again, and sat waiting for him.

At last, she heard him approach. She stood up and, just before he stepped into the room, she began to yell as she stomped her feet in a dance of rage. She rolled her eyes, shook her head fiercely, and cried, "WHY DID YOU STEAL MY FISH AND MANGOES, YOU MISERABLE MAN?"

Gopi started to shake; his guilt made him weak with fright. He put his hands together and fell at her feet, pleading, "Forgive me, goddess, forgive me!"

"I SHOULD DESTROY YOU RIGHT NOW!" shouted his goddess-wife.

"Oh, please, give me a chance. I'll do anything for you," Gopi cried.

"SINCE YOUR WIFE IS SO KIND, I'LL SHOW MERCY TO YOU. TAKE THE POT WITH THE CURRY TO MY TEMPLE AT ONCE. THROW IT IN THE TANK, AND I WILL FORGIVE YOU!"

Gopi quickly picked up the pot and ran without stopping to the tank. He tossed the pot far into the tank, then returned home. When he walked into the house, he saw his wife on the floor, her eyes closed.

"Kamala, are you all right?" he asked gently, relieved that the goddess had left his wife.

Slowly, she opened her eyes, as if awakening from a deep sleep. She looked around the room, then at him, and at last she spoke. "What happened? Why am I on the floor? Why is my hair wet? And where is the fish curry?"

Fools

Stories of fools, past and present, are found frequently in South India. These fools try to push buildings, get on the wrong trains, make silly bets, and do many more witless acts. Some fool tales poke fun at religious figures and others in authority, as in this tale of the well-known Guru Paramanandaiah and his silly disciples.

Crossing the River

One day, a guru and his nine followers were on their way to a temple when they reached a large river. They wanted to cross it after eating, so they started a fire, then cooked and ate some rice.

"Now we must cross the river," said the guru. "But first we should see if it is awake. This is a powerful river, and we can only go across when it is sleeping." He ordered one follower to test the river. The man took a hot stick from the fire and ran to the river. When he placed it in the water, it made a loud HISSSSSS.

"Ah," he shouted to the others. "The river is still very much awake. It talks loudly and sounds quite fierce."

"Well, let us sleep and let the river rest, too," said the wise guru. "In the morning perhaps we can cross." Soon snores crept through the air as the night passed. At dawn, another man was sent to check the river. The stick he took was dry and cold because the fire had gone out long ago. When he thrust it in the river, he heard not a sound.

"We can cross," he whispered as he tiptoed back. "The river is asleep and very quiet now."

Thus the band of fools crossed the sleeping river. At the other side, the guru looked around and said, "Let us make sure that we have all reached safely." And he counted his group. However, since he didn't count himself, he counted only nine people.

"Wait," he cried. "One of us is missing. The river must have eaten him." He began to sob. The others counted but, making the same mistake, they each found nine as well. As they all cried, a man walked by and asked the problem. When he heard, he looked carefully at the fools, then said, "I believe that I can find your lost friend. But I will need a reward—it is a difficult task."

Eagerly they gave him all the money they had.

"Now," he said. "Close your eyes while I work. When I am finished with my magic, I will touch each of you and you must count out loud." The fools closed their eyes and waited. At last, each felt a sharp hit upon his back and so they shouted, one after another, "One-nu, rendu, moonu, nalu, anji, arru, yerru, ettu, onpadu, pattu."

"I have found him. There are ten of you here now. Good luck as you journey on," shouted the man as he walked away, grinning.

"What a wise man," cried the men. "How wonderful to be reunited." With great smiles, the ten fools traveled on, all together again.

A Modern Fool

An American tourist, who spoke no Hindi, came to see the sights in Delhi. His pleasant taxi driver took him first to the grand Jama Masjid.

"Beautiful," gushed the American. "Who built it?"

"*Bata nay,*" ("I don't know,") replied the driver. On they went to the great Red Fort of the Moghuls, constructed centuries ago.

"Magnificent," raved the American. "And who built that?"

"Bata nay," replied the driver.

Then at the large, impressive India Gate, the American marveled again, asking, "Do you know who built this?" He received the same reply, "Bata nay."

All of a sudden, they heard sad cries and the sound of a loud drum. They saw several lines of people marching on the street, with some carrying a flower-covered body on a stretcher.

"What is that?" asked the American. The driver made a gesture meaning death.

"Do you know who died?"

"Bata nay."

"Oh, that's really too bad," sighed the American. "Poor Mr. Bata Nay. He was a very talented man, and such a great builder too. What a shame that he had to die just now."

Modern Jokes

Jokes are some of the most commonly told stories in India today. They take less time to tell and help listeners deal with the tensions in modern Indian life. There are jokes about family planning, the telephone system, traffic, power cuts, adulterated food, corruption, religion, the government, and more. Yet although there are many modern jokes in South India, not all can be easily told in the United States. A number are told about Indian political figures and make no sense to outsiders. Others depend upon puns impossible to translate, while some are told by or about a minority group and thus inappropriate here. Try the jokes below that do give a sample of contemporary South Indian humor.

One Sad Story

Three students, from the United States, France, and India, once stayed together in an apartment on the top floor of a very tall Indian building. They shared one key that the Indian student usually kept because he returned first every day. One afternoon, though, they all arrived at the front door together. They walked inside and pushed the elevator button. Nothing happened. Then they noticed that the lights were out.

"Ah," said the American. "Another power cut. We'll have to walk up." And so they began to climb the sixty steep flights of stairs. To pass the time, the Frenchman told a love story that made them sigh for twenty flights. Next, the American told an adventure tale that gave them energy during the next twenty flights. The Indian then began a tale from South Indian history and finished it just below their floor.

"Well, we have time for one more short, sad story," he said as they huffed up the last few stairs.

"What story?" asked the American, breathing painfully.

"A true story to make you cry," replied the Indian. "I left the key at my college."

The Shy Soldier

A man was feeling shy to join the army. Do you know why?
If he joined the army, two things could happen:

- he could fight in a war zone, or go to a peace zone. If in a peace zone, no problem,
- but if he fought in a war zone, two things could happen:
- he could live or he could die. If he lived, no problem,
- but if he died, two things could happen:
- he could be buried or cremated. If cremated, no problem,
- but if buried, two things could happen:
- he could turn into coal or petroleum. If coal, no problem,
- but if petroleum, two things could happen:
- he could turn into laundry soap or bath soap. If laundry soap, no problem,
- but if bath soap, two things could happen:
- he could turn into gent's soap or lady's soap. If gent's soap, no problem,
- but if lady's soap, he would have to touch a lady's skin while she bathed.

And that's why he was feeling shy to join the army!

Thin Milk

One day in Chennai, the milk that used to be so thin and watery was suddenly delivered to housewives in a rich, creamy form. Days passed with such delicious milk while people wondered at the change. Saraswati, a hard-working housewife, grew more and more curious about the new, better milk. Finally one morning she stopped the delivery boy.

"What happened?" she asked. "Your milk used to be so weak and watered down. Now it's thick and rich. Why?"

"Madam," he replied sadly. "It's not our fault. We want to sell it to you nice and watery like we used to, because then we make a good profit. Yet now with this cursed drought and the water shortage, we can't get any water to mix with the milk, to thin it down. But don't worry; after the rains come, your milk will be back to normal!"

The Making of a Sword

An American, a Russian, and an Indian were working together once in a metal factory. One day, the American made a good, sharp sword blade and showed it proudly to the others. Next, the Russian went to his workbench, sculpted a wonderful sword handle, and attached it firmly to the sword. The Indian, not knowing what else he could add, thought for a moment, then quickly picked up the sword and carved across the blade in large letters, "Made in India."

Appendix

South Indian Festivals

Indian festivals, rich in color, light, faith, and art, are frequent and well enjoyed. There are celebrations of national pride, festivals to honor gods, harvest festivals, local temple festivals, and much more. Festivals are traditionally important as ways to unite the population, often going beyond divisions of religion, caste, community, and language. They also help craftspeople who make and sell traditional statues and decorations needed for certain festivals.

When the god of a temple is worshipped, the image is given special treatment, as Chettiar describes: "The main deity is dressed in colorful costumes and adorned with very valuable and rare jewelry, mounted on special carts and taken round the temple in processions . . . to enable the sick, the old, the disabled, to get a direct view of the deity and to offer prayers" (Chettiar 1980, 94).

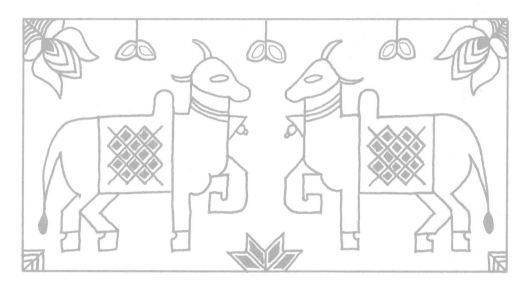

Two festive cows in a Pongal kolam.

Many important ceremonies and rituals are also performed within the family, although their celebration depends upon region, caste, and finances. In many Hindu households, rituals and fasts are done to protect a family member, for puberty, for marriage, to welcome a baby, for a child's growth, and to remember the dead. Fairs and carnivals are also popular—traditional market fairs and fairs linked to religious festivals as well as the newer book fairs, handloom fairs, and trade fairs that attract large, eager crowds.

A few of the major South Indian festivals are noted below so that you can use one as a special time to share a South Indian tale. The Indian calendar is a complicated one that uses both solar and lunar calculations; thus, festival dates on a Western calendar vary each year for many festivals. Check with resource sites listed later to find specific dates for the current year.

Pongal (January 13-16)

a harvest festival, is the most popular holiday in Tamil Nadu. Houses are cleaned and whitewashed, with festive bonfires made of old things. New clothes are worn and the house is decorated with kolams, mango leaves, and flower hangings. The sun is worshipped and special foods are made, especially *pongal*, a mixture that overflows its pot to symbolize overflowing fields. After that, cows are decorated and worshipped, while the last day is set aside for visiting and relaxing. January 14 is also celebrated, with much happiness, as *Makara Sankranti* festival in parts of Karnataka and Andhra Pradesh.

Republic Day (January 26)

honors the day that India became a republic in 1950.

Sivaratri (February-March)

is a religious festival in honor of Siva. Devotees fast as they spend the night singing his praise and worshipping his image.

New Year's Day (April)

is celebrated on two different dates in the south, depending on the state.

Independence Day (August 15)

marks the day of freedom from British rule.

Janmashtami (July-August)

celebrates the birth of Krishna through worship and devotional singing. In some places, scenes from his life are shared through models, games, plays, or stories.

Ganesha (or Vinayaka) Chaturthi (August-September)
celebrates the birth of Ganesha. Clay models of the god are purchased or made; he is worshipped, especially with the sweets he loves; and then the models are immersed in water.

Onam (August-September)
the most popular holiday in Kerala, is celebrated after the crops have been harvested. It marks the yearly visit of the beloved former king, Mahabali, from his underground kingdom. Beautiful flower creations are made, new clothes are worn, happy visiting is done, and, in some areas, boat races are enjoyed.

Dussera (September-October)
is a time to honor Rama, especially in Mysore, where thousands of lights on the palace, finely decorated elephants, and a grand parade are part of the celebration.

Deepawali (October-November)
began with lamps lit to celebrate Lord Krishna's victory over a demon. Today the holiday is enjoyed with festive lights, sweets, visits, and fireworks.

Navaratri (October-November)
is celebrated for nine nights in honor of the goddess in her different forms. Delightful *kolus* (displays of dolls) are made, and friends happily visit each other as well as the temple.

Karthigai Deepam (November-December)
is the festival of lights celebrated especially in Tamil Nadu and Andhra Pradesh.

Christmas (December 25)
is joyfully celebrated by Indian Christians in churches and family gatherings.

The Islamic calendar, a lunar calendar of 354 days, shows even more variance from the Western calendar than does the Hindu calendar. Thus, over a period of years, holidays move throughout the different seasons. Sources in the resource section can help you find current dates for these important Muslim holidays:

Eid-al-Fitr
is a joyous celebration to mark the end of Ramadan, the Muslim month of fasting.

Bakr-Eid
commemorates the sacrifice of Abraham.

Unadorned temple cart, Andhra Pradesh. Photo courtesy of Rajani Bommakanti.

Resources

The addresses below can help you locate resources for home, school, or library. There are also South Asia outreach centers located at several major universities that provide excellent materials for schools. For up-to-date information about a center near you, contact AskAsia or *Teaching About Asia*, both listed below.

Asia Society
725 Park Ave.
New York, NY 10021
Phone: 888-ASK-ASIA
Fax: 888-FAX-ASIA
URL: www.askasia.org
    AskAsia help and publications.

Association for Asian Studies
1021 E. Huron St.
Ann Arbor, MI 48104
Phone: 313-665-2490
E-mail: postmaster@aasianst.org
    Order *Teaching About Asia* magazine.

Government of India Tourism
30 Rockefeller Plaza
15 North Mezzanine
New York, NY 10020
Phone: 212-586-4901
    Information on India.

Heritage Key
6102 E. Mescal St.
Scottsdale, AZ 85254-5419
Phone: 602-483-3313
Fax: 602-483-9666
    A catalog that lists Indian books, dolls, and games.

KAZI Publications
3023-27 W. Belmont Ave.
Chicago, IL 60618
Phone: 773-267-7001
Fax: 773-267-7002

E-mail: Kazibooks@kazi.org
URL: www.kazi.org
    Send for the Islam and the Muslim World Catalog.

Marketplace: Handwork of India
1455 Ashland Ave.
Evanston, IL 60201-4001
Phone: 800-726-8905
    Order Indian clothes and crafts.

Sangeet Natak Akademi
Rabindra Bhavan
Feroze Shah Rd.
New Delhi, India 110001
    Find publications on Indian performing arts.

Shen's Books and Supplies
8625 Hubbard Rd.
Auburn, CA 95602-7815
Phone: 800-456-6660
Local Phone: 530-888-6776
Fax: 530-888-6763
    Receive a catalog of multicultural books.

South Asia Books
P.O. Box 502
Columbia, MO 65205
E-mail: sab@socketis.net
    An extensive catalog of Indian books is available.

For a class project, consider fund-raising for . . .

ASHA
asha-info@cs.stanford.edu
URL: http://www.ashanet.org
Started by concerned college students, ASHA now has groups across the United States helping to raise funds for basic education in India.

Child Relief & You (CRY)
120 Deepwood Dr.
Hamden, CT 06517
Phone: 203-785-8005
CRY has sponsored more than 150 grassroots projects in India since 1979, including work with vocational and nonformal education, maternal and child health, disabled children, and child laborers.

The India Network Foundation Inc.
P.O. Box 556
Bowling Green, OH 43402
Phone/Fax: 419-352-9335
URL: www.indnet.org
This foundation runs a useful on-line Indian news service and discussion group, funds education projects, and helps with emergency relief.

People for Progress in India
P.O. Box 51231
Seattle, WA 98115-1231
This organization funds varied development projects in India, including reforestation, education, vocational training, crafts production, and more.

For pen pals in India . . .

Amity International
45-40-36/2 Abid Nagar
Vishakhapatnam 530 016
A.P., India

International Penpal Club
Radio Bhavan
3/35 Kamal Mansion
Arthur Bunder Rd.
Colaba
Mumbai 400 005
Maharashtra, India

WCF's International PenFriends
World Cultural Foundation
P.O. Box 1129
Snoqualmie, WA 98065-1129
URL: www.wcf.org

World Pen Pal
17914 123 Ct. S.E.
Renton, WA 98058
Phone: 206-271-8366

South India on the Internet

Deccan Chronicle. *Deccan Chronicle.* ©1996. Available: http://www. deccan.com. (Accessed July 17, 1998).
Deccan Chronicle is the largest circulated English daily newspaper from Hyderabad, India.

GENIUS Technologies, Inc. *Welcome to INDOlink: Your Electronic Link to India, and Indian Communities World-Wide!* ©1995–1998. Available: http://www.genius.net/ indolink; *also at* http://www.

indolink.com. (Accessed July 17, 1998).
Quiz, recipes, even meanings of baby's names.

Himalayan Academy. 1997. *Tirukkural.* ©1994. Available: http://www.ece. utexas.edu/~janahan/kural/kural-body.html. (Accessed July 17, 1998).
The *Tirukkural* online.

hNr Corporation. *Vista India: The Premier Indian Music Source.* ©1997. Available: http://www. vmo.com. (Accessed July 17, 1998).
Vista mail order for Karnatic music tapes and CDs (also available by phone: 908-494-9155).

Ibrahim Shafi. n.d. *The Islam Page.* Available: http://www.islamworld. net. (Accessed July 17, 1998).
The Islam Page, with resources of every description about Islam.

Indian Express Newspapers (Bombay) Ltd. *Net Express: The Web Site of the Indian Express Group.* ©1998. Available: http://www. expressindia.com. (Accessed July 17, 1998).
Indian Express newspaper online.

IndiaWorld Communications Pvt. Ltd. *INDIAWORLD: India's Largest Internet Family.* ©1995–1998. Available: http://www.indiaworld. co.in. (Accessed July 17, 1998).
Gateway to various news articles and information on Indian publications.

InfoHub. *InfoHub: Specialty Travel Guide.* ©1995. Available: http: //www.infohub.com/TRAVEL/ TRAVELLER/ASIA/india.html. (Accessed July 17, 1998).
Master list of many links, including Indian state sites.

ISOL, Inc. *IndiaOnline: Your Link to the Indian Subcontinent.* ©1995– 1997. Available: http://www. indiaonline.com. (Accessed July 17, 1998).
Good general information on festivals and tourism.

Ministry of External Affairs. n.d. *India: Culture: Literature.* Available: http: //www.meadev.gov.in/culture/ literature/intro.htm; *also try* http: //www.meadev.gov.in. (Accessed July 17, 1998).
Fine resource on modern Indian writing, includes material on South Indian writers.

Navrang Inc. n.d. *Navrang Inc.* Available: http://catalog.com/navrang. (Accessed July 17, 1998).
Source of Indian books and more.

Ossai Internet. *Tamils' Web: Bringing the Tamil World Together.* ©1994–1998. Available: http: //www.tamil.org/aboutus.html. (Accessed July 17, 1998).
Lots of links on Tamil culture worldwide.

Panalink Internet Services. *IndiaConnect.* ©1997. Available: http:// www.indiaconnect.com/index. htm. (Accessed July 17, 1998).
Indian news, astrology, games, pen pals, and more.

South Asian Milan. *Welcome to South Asian Milan: Your Online Resource to the Countries, Cultures and Communities of South Asia.* ©1997–1998. Available: http://www.samilan.com. (Accessed July 17, 1998).

Search engine for resources on India and South Asia.

SAWNEWS: News About South Asian Women. 1998. Available: http://www.umiacs.umd.edu/users/sawweb/sawnet/news.html. (Accessed July 17, 1998).

Many items on South Asian women.

Soaked rice is ground with a stone mortar and pestle to make dosa (rice pancake) batter, Tamil Nadu © Lou Corbett.

Glossary

This glossary includes words used at least twice and those not defined in the text.

ashram—a hermitage, also at times a place of religious instruction

asuras—beings who do not believe in God, but believe in their own power and might

Bhagavati—powerful form of the Goddess, popular in Kerala

bhakti—religious devotion

bhutas—spirits worshipped, especially in South Karnataka

Brahman—the Supreme, the Almighty in Hindu thought

Brahmin—the highest caste in Hinduism; priests come from this caste

Burra Katha—form of three-person storytelling famous in Andhra Pradesh

caste—a division in traditional Hindu society

Chakyar Kuttu—sophisticated form of storytelling in Kerala; performed in temples

Chitra Katha—form of storytelling using pictures in sequence

devas—heavenly beings

dharma—doing what is right; also one's duty

dhoti—long piece of white cloth wrapped around man's waist and worn instead of pants

Ganesha—popular elephant-headed Hindu god, the remover of obstacles and the son of Siva; also called Ganapati or Vinayaka

guru—teacher

Hajj—pilgrimage to Makkah (Mecca), to be done at least once in the life of a Muslim, if circumstances permit

Harijan—*Children of God*—word coined by Gandhi to replace the word "untouchable," which describes those at the bottom of the caste system

Harikatha—difficult musical storytelling style

incarnation—a form taken in one lifetime

Jains—a religious group, known for their nonviolence, whose most important saint was Mahavira

kalamkari—hand-painted cloth famous in Andhra Pradesh; used at times for storytelling

kalaripayattu—martial art of Kerala

Kali—very powerful form of the goddess; especially popular in Kerala

karma—the fruits of one's actions; usually seen in future lifetimes

Kathaprasangam—musical storytelling in Kerala, without religious messages or themes

kolam—drawing on street or floor; also called *muggu* or *rangoli*

Kolam

Krishna—popular incarnation of Lord Vishnu; plays a role in epic *Mahabharata*

Kutiyattam—oldest existing Sanskrit (language) drama in India; found only in Kerala

lungi—long piece of colored cloth often stitched into tube, tucked around man's waist and worn instead of pants

mantra—sacred words that give power when spoken; also a chant to be repeated for meditation

masjid—place of worship for Muslims

moksha—spiritual release; the last of the four traditional goals in life for Hindus

mudras—elegant hand sign language used in classical Indian dance and in Ottan Thullal (see below)

Muhammad—the final Prophet of God in Islam religion

Muslim—one who follows Islam, believing in: Allah and the unseen; Qur'an (Koran) and revealed books; Prophet Muhammad and prophets before him; correct prayers, fasting, Hajj, and charity

Ottan Thullal—storytelling form from Kerala, with costume, dance, satire, and music

panchayat—village-level governing body

puja—worship directed to a god, the sun, a sacred tree . . . done with flowers, water, fire, song, ritual, prayer, and various offerings

raga—melody-like structure in Indian music; usually associated with a time of day and mood

raja—king; maharaja means "great king"

Rama—an incarnation of Vishnu and hero of the epic *Ramayana*

rani—queen; maharani means "great queen"

Ravana—the 10-headed monster who kidnapped Sita and fought Rama in the *Ramayana*

rupee—unit of Indian money

salvar kameez—two-piece outfit for females, with long flowing top over pants

sari—woman's dress made from one long piece of cotton, silk, or polyester, wrapped around body over blouse and underskirt

Sita—Rama's wife; symbol of devotion and courage; from *Ramayana*

Siva—a major Hindu god; known for his meditation on Mt. Kailasa and for his cosmic dance

Sri—term of respect used before men's names, Srimati is used before women's names. Sri is also a name for the goddess Lakshmi

Subramanyam—son of Siva, and a very popular god in South India; also called Kartikeya or Skanda, or known as Murugan, who was first an older Tamil god

tala—beats or a rhythmic cycle in Indian music

tambura—simple stringed instrument used in Indian music and in some storytelling traditions

tapas—great penance or hardship undergone to receive boons

Villu Pattu—storytelling form in southern Tamil Nadu and Kerala, with large musical bow

Vishnu—an important Hindu god; known in 10 major incarnations; the best-known are Krishna and Rama

Notes on Story Sources and Motifs

Librarians, storytellers, and folklore scholars who share stories often wish to compare stories and study story themes. One tool useful for classification and comparison of story parts is the folklore motif, collected most extensively in the six-volume *Motif-Index of Folk Literature* (Thompson 1955-1958). To explore folklore collections for children through this scheme, see *The Storyteller's Sourcebook* (MacDonald 1982).

Another tool for folklore study is the Tale Type Index created by Finnish folklorist Antti Aarne and updated with Thompson (Aarne and Thompson 1961). In this index, tales are classified by a tale type number with a description (e.g., Cinderella is 510A). Several adaptations of these works were made using early Indian folklore collections:

Heda, Jason. *Types of Indic Oral Tales Supplement*. Helsinki: Academia Scientiarum Fennica, 1989.

Thompson, Stith, and Jonas Baylys. *The Oral Tales of India*. Westport, CT: Greenwood Press, 1976.

Thompson, Stith, and Warren E. Roberts. *Types of Indic Oral Tales: India, Pakistan and Ceylon*. Helsinki: Suomalainen Tiedeakatemia, 1960.

Below, we have included motifs from Thompson and tale types from Aarne/Thompson because they will be of use to many who read this. However, a word of caution by noted Indian scholar A. K. Ramanujan may also be of interest:

> These indexes, however useful, were made in the 1950s and 1960s and are based on outdated theories. The Indian index was made without access to collections in the regional languages. . . . The collection of folktales in some of the mother tongues of India has begun again only in the last few decades. So many of the tales in these recent books do not find any mention in the indexes (Ramanujan 1991, 323).

"Serving with Care"

Paramasivam has told me this more than any other tale, perhaps because he finds himself often upset at all the waste in the United States.

Motifs include W216 *Thrift*.

"The Greedy Guest"

This I adapted from retellings in *Tales of Tamil Nadu* (Rajamanickam 1985) and *Folk Tales of Tamilnadu* (Seethalakshmi 1986). It is a fun tale to tell, similar to the American favorite "Old Dry Frye" in Richard Chase's *Grandfather Tales*, but with a different surprise twist in the ending.

A/T Type 1536 *Disposing of a corpse*. Motifs include W125 *Gluttony*.

"Soma and Bhima"

Shree Coorg shared this tale with me in 1997 in Seattle. Her father told it to her when she was growing up in Karnataka. Many Indian proverbs and sayings also warn against greed. One of our family favorites is from Gandhi: "The Earth has enough for everyone's needs, but not enough for everyone's greeds."

A/T Type 729 *Ax lost in the river*. Motifs include F343.18 *Fairies return hatchet head lost in river*; Q 68.2 *Honesty rewarded*.

"Great Wealth, Great Pride"

I heard this from student teachers at Balar Kalvi Nilayam school, Chennai, in 1983.

A/T Type 836 *Pride is punished*. Motifs include L412 *Rich man made poor to punish*; W151 *Greed*.

"Lives of the Prophets"

Both Paramasivam and I know relatively little about the rich Muslim traditions in South India. So the Council for Islamic Education, California, referred me to Omar Khalidi, who grew up in Hyderabad. Because he remembered often hearing tales of the prophets, I adapted these two short, well-known anecdotes from *Stories from Prophet's Life* (Rauf 1990).

A/T Type 967 *Man saved by a spider web over refuge*.

"Worship of Great and Small"

When Paramasivam and I went to the grand temple in Thanjavur in 1985, a guide told us this legend. There are many such tales that praise the faith of a humble devotee, and there are also many tales about the origins of temples.

Motifs include Q20 *Piety rewarded*; V112 *Temples*.

"Druva"

I heard this during an interview in 1984 with Ramasubramaniya Sarma, a kind and humorous storyteller living in Chennai, and from educator Indira Seshagiri Rao in Hyderabad. It is well known not only in Harikatha but also through many oral and printed versions in India.

Motifs include Q22 *Reward for faith.*

"The Great Battle"

While hunting down Teyyam rituals in Kerala in 1985, I heard this popular story from my talented guide and friend, artist Krishna Kumar Marar. Since then, I have seen it acted and danced in various rituals in Kerala.

Motifs include Q115 *Reward: any boon that may be asked*; Z310 *Unique vulnerability.*

"A Tale of Dharma"

Paramasivam remembers hearing this at a local temple as a boy when they had yearly tellings of the *Mahabharata* or *Ramayana*. The most faithful listeners were the elders who came every day, while he and his friends spent more time running through the temple grounds than listening. But they did hear bits and pieces, including this popular small story from the end of the *Mahabharata*.

Motifs include A2493.4 *Friendship between man and dog*; Q72 *Loyalty rewarded.*

"What Is Real?"

Paramasivam heard this several times from a good friend, modern artist M. V. Devan from Kerala, who is also known for his writing and his creative, low-cost building designs.

Motifs include K1827 *Disguise as holy man*; R350 *Recapture of fugitive.*

"The Right Time"

I heard this in the Ramakrishna Mission in Chennai in 1993. Sri Ramakrishna was a famous saint from Bengal, North India, who is also well respected in the south. Across India are many missions where his teachings are shared and much social service done. His parables and short stories are clear and clever, often making difficult truths easy to understand.

Motifs include Q143 *Superior reincarnation as reward.*

"Telling the Future"

Paramasivam heard this as a child and often told it to me to teach both about Indian astrology and the importance of detail.

Motifs include M302.4 *Horoscope taken by means of stars*; M311 *Prophecy: Future greatness of unborn child.*

"Who Will Win?"

This is one of Paramasivam's favorite tales. He often told it to our son, Manu, when he was younger. Many tales are told of Ganesha, a most popular god, the remover of obstacles. Although he is also called by other names in the south, we used his most common name so that you can recognize him again in other Indian stories.

Motifs include Q65 *Filial duty rewarded.*

"A Devoted Son"

One day a painter from Kalahasti, A. P., a town famous for *kalamkari* cloth, came to our home in Cholamandal, Chennai. In his bag he had long pieces of wonderful painted cloth. He spread them out and told us many of the tales behind them. We never learned his name, but we heard this well-known story from the *Ramayana*, then bought the cloth with the tale. A version with a happier ending is found in *Seasons of Splendour* (Jaffrey, 1985, 16-20).

Motifs include M414.5 *King cursed*; P230 *Parents and children*; V 530 *Pilgrimage.*

"Strange Fruit"

I heard this story from Lily Kunnath, the wife of my guide and host in central Kerala.

Motifs include N113.1 *Good fortune resides in an object*; N817 *Deity as helper*; P262.1 *Bad relations between mother-in-law and daughter-in-law.*

"My Son, Your Son"

A dear friend and an inspiring educator, Professor Rastogi, told me this in New Delhi after having heard it from a friend in Andhra Pradesh.

"A Teacher's Skill"

This brief tale was shared in a teachers' workshop in Chennai in 1994. In general, Indian children have a great deal of respect for teachers and elders. They are expected to—they have heard many tales and proverbs reminding them of its importance. The story is also found as "Amba Jataka" in *The Jataka* (Cowell, 1973, vol. 4, 124-128).

Motifs include P340 *Teacher and pupil*.

"Yes Dear, Do"

I heard this lovely tale in Chennai from a fine freedom fighter, journalist, and folklore collector there, Mugavai Rajamanickam. A different version is the "Clay Mother-in-law" (Ramanujan 1991, 30-33).

A/T Type 1653 *Robbers under the tree. Object falls, they flee and leave money.*

"The Loyal Parrot"

I heard this at a storytelling workshop for teachers in Mysore, 1988. I later found it as "Mahasuka Jataka" (Cowell 1973, vol. 3, 291-293).

Motifs include P310 *Friendship*; Q72 *Loyalty rewarded*; Q115 *Reward—any boon that may be asked.*

"A Guest Is Always Welcome"

Paramasivam remembers this from childhood when the importance of hospitality was often impressed upon him. The story is also told about Appar, one of the Nayanmar saints who worshipped Siva. When the boy is called in that version, Appar sings a most lovely song, counting from one to ten while naming attributes and qualities of Lord Siva. When the song is finished, the boy returns to life (Vanmikanathan 1985).

A/T Type 750B *Hospitality rewarded*. Motifs include E121.4 *Resuscitation by saint*; Q45 *Hospitality rewarded*.

"Krishna and Sudama"

Paramasivam remembers hearing this as a boy, and it is also found in the *Bhagavata Purana*, a famous collection of myths about Krishna. The theme of divine blessing is echoed in a Jaina story, when a wife sends her husband to ask her father for financial help, wrapping a little chickpea flour for a gift. But on the way he gives it to a Jaina monk. After an unsuccessful visit at his in-law's, he fills a small bag of pebbles to cheer up his wife and heads home. But when she empties the bag, they have turned to precious jewels, for such is the power of charity, especially to holy ones (Pratham 1984).

Motifs include N817 *Deity as helper*; P324.1 *Host treats guest with food and everything possible*; Q22 *Reward for faith*.

"A Pot of Dreams"

Paramasivam heard this when younger and passes it on still today. It is a very common type of tale around the world because many people find it easier to dream than to work!

A/T Type 1430 *Man and his wife build air castles*. Motifs include J2061.2 *Air castle: pail of milk to be sold*.

"King's Questions"

I heard this from P. R. Thippeswamy, an artist and friend in Mysore, in 1984. A Laotian version, "Are We All Equal?" is found in Naomi Wakan's *Telling Tales on the Rim* (Victoria, BC: Pacific-Rim Publishers, 1995, 131-133).

Motifs include Q85 *Reward for asking proper questions*.

"Mouse Merchant"

Manu and I first discovered this in a very popular Indian comic magazine, *Tinkle,* years ago. It is similar to "The Straw Choja" in Japan and to many versions worldwide of this lucky exchange chain story. I later found the story both as "Cullaka-Setthi Jataka," (Cowell 1973, vol. 1, 14-17) and in the famous classic collection of Indian tales, *Katha Sarit Sagara* (Tawney 1968, vol. 1, 33-34).

A/T Type 1655 *Profitable exchanges*. Motifs include N421.1 *Progressive lucky bargains*; Q86 *Reward for industry*.

"The Guru"

In 1993, I had the honor of going to a *kalari* in Thiruvananthapuram to watch the amazing training that went on. This was after a wonderful conversation with Sri Kavalam Narayana Panikkar, a most gifted director from Kerala. During our time together, he told me this anecdote. I then found more details in *Legends of Kerala* (Nair 1976, 21-27).

Motifs include Q66 *Humility rewarded*; Q86 *Reward for industry*.

"The Squirrel's Stripes"

This short tale is one Paramasivam has told me from time to time. It is a side story in the famous *Ramayana* and is a lovely little "how and why" tale.

Motifs include A2221.8 *Squirrel's markings as reward by deity*.

"The Elephant King"

This story is one of over 550 *Jatakas* that portray the past lives of the Lord Buddha. These stories were earlier told by Buddhist monks but now are shared in

India primarily through books and illustrated comics. I began retelling this tale, the "Chaddanta Jataka," years ago in India, adapting it from several versions there of the *Jatakas*. Strangely enough, after we decided to include it, we discovered that it was one of the *Jatakas* carved in the stupa at Amaravati, Andhra Pradesh (Dehajia 1990).

Motifs include F127.2 *Journey to land of elephants*; W28 *Self-sacrifice*.

"King Kumanan"

One day while visiting some friends in Chennai for the holiday of Navaratri, I saw several stories of just and kind kings shown in a model display made for the holiday. Shantha, the young woman who made it, told me this story, among others. There is still a great deal of pride in South India about such just rulers from the past. Their stories are sometimes contrasted with stories of modern politicians, and you can guess who seems the best!

Motifs include P12.6 *Just king brings good fortune upon people*; P16.1 *King retires from world*; Q91.3 *King rewards poem*.

"The Bell of Justice"

Such tools of justice were found in various South Indian kingdoms in years past, and their stories were widely shared. We adapted this version from *Folk Tales of Andhra Pradesh* (Rama Raju 1981) for use with younger children. A better-known version is the story of Manu Neethi Cholan, for whom our son was named: A cow once rang the bell of this just king and showed the dead body of her calf. The king demanded that whoever had killed the calf must give his life, even when he found out that his own son had run over the calf, in the royal chariot. The boy was bound and placed on the road to be run over, when suddenly a voice from the sky ordered the boy freed because he had not seen the calf. The boy was released, and everyone praised a king so just that he was ready to sacrifice his own son.

A/T Type 207C *Bell of justice*. Motifs include B271.3 *Animals ring bell and demand justice*.

"Avvaiyar's Rest"

Tales and sayings of this famous poet-sage are common in Tamil Nadu; I heard this story so often over the years that I can't recall who first told it to me. Rajagopalachari includes it in his collection of her poems (Rajagopalachari 1971). To prove Avvaiyar's worth, our friend Indira Seshagiri Rao told me of a Tamil king, Adhiyamaan, who underwent hardship to find a special fruit that kept illness away and grew only once every 12 years. Because of his goodness, he wished to give the fruit to a deserving person rather than to eat it himself. He finally gave it to Avvaiyar, deciding that her life best served humanity.

"Obavva of the Pestle"

I heard this from P. R. Thippeswamy in Mysore and read it in several Indian books years ago. In Seattle recently, Shree Coorg from Karnataka shared it with me as well, urging me to use it to inspire us all.

Motifs include L113.4 *Peasant as hero*.

"Resisting the British: Rani Channamma"

Such stories about freedom fighters are widely known in South India. I have heard about these heroes from countless friends and acquaintances; the stories are a source of pride. I found details about Rani Channamma in Mysore earlier and recently in *Women Freedom Fighters in Karnataka* (Shintri and Rao 1983). For any readers who reach India, a visit to the Gandhi Memorial Museum, in Madurai, offers one of the most moving ways to learn the stories of India's long fight for freedom.

"Ramanujan"

The story of this mathematical genius is another source of pride to modern South Indians. A recent biography, *The Man Who Knew Infinity* (Kanigel 1991), gives much fascinating detail about his remarkable talent and perseverance. To write his story, Manu used that book along with a number of articles published during Ramanujan's birth centenary (1987) and afterwards. A good friend, Dr. Ramesh Gangolli, told us the true story of 1729, which is a well-known anecdote about Ramanujan.

"Tenali Raman"

Tenali Raman is beloved in South India under this name or a close variant. Many know his stories; they are shared by mouth, in books, through comics, and over the television. The tale of the yawn was told by Rajalakshmi, a young girl in Chennai, in 1990. The tale of sugar was told by G. Latha in Chennai, while the tale of the mangoes I have heard from many people. Versions of the mango tale, along with other tales of this jester, are found in the Indian folktale collections of Ramanujan (1991) and Beck et al. (1987). See also *The King and the Clown in South Indian Myth and Poetry* (Shulman 1985) for a more involved discussion of Tenali Raman's role.

A/T Type 1539: *Tricksters and their victims*. Motifs include H561.5 *King and clever minister*; J1124 *Clever court jester*.

"A Real Bargain"

This tale, one of the many told by Urdu speakers in India, came to me from artist Sultan Ali, who lived in Cholamandal and was very proud of his Muslim culture. For more tales of this fine trickster, see the various collections by Idries Shah.

Motifs include AT921D *Witty responses*.

"The Fish Curry"

This very tellable tale I adapted years ago from *Tales from a South Indian Village* (Nilakanta 1973, 36-40), and I recently found a version in *Tales of the Sun* (Kingscote and Sastri 1890 [repr. 1977], 257-261).

Motifs include K1969.4.1 *Posing as deity*; W125.2 *Gluttonous wife eats all the meal*.

"Crossing the River"

K. S. Gopal, a good friend and artist who died at too early an age, told me this one day at Cholamandal. Fools around the world seem to have trouble crossing rivers and counting themselves. There are many stories of this Guru Paramanandaiah and his not-so-clever followers. He is known in both South India and Sri Lanka by various names. Another Indian version is found in Ramanujan (1991, 157-159).

A/T Type 1287 *Fools cannot count themselves*. Motifs include J2031 *Counting wrong by not counting oneself*.

"A Modern Fool"

Rajalakshmi, our young friend in Chennai who was learning Hindi, told us this joke. Hindi is the national language of India and is taught in most South Indian schools today.

A/T Type 1700 *"I don't know."*

"One Sad Story"

This came from Maya Thiagarajan, our favorite joke teller in Chennai and a rich source of popular jokes, in 1994. Maya was 12 years old when she told this.

"The Shy Soldier"

A fun chain joke from young Rajalakshmi in Chennai. It is best told by those with good memories!

A/T Type 2014 *Chains involving contradictions*.

"Thin Milk"

Our friend G. Latha told me this little joke when we were in Chennai in 1993. Like many jokes, there is truth behind it, both about the problem of adulterated food and the water shortages that plague Chennai from time to time.

"The Making of a Sword"

This also came from Maya Thiagarajan, age 12, in 1994.

Working elephant, Kerala.

Bibliography

For Adults

Aarne, Antti, and Stith Thompson. 1961. *The Types of the Folktale.* Helsinki: Suomalainen Tiedeakatemia.

Adigal, Prince Ilango. 1965. *Shilappadikaram.* New York: New Directions.

Allen, Charles, and Sharada Dwivedi. 1984. *Lives of the Indian Princes.* New York: Crown.

Alvares, Claude. "The Genius of Hindu Civilization." *Illustrated Weekly of India* (June 15, 1986).

Ayyar, K. V. Krishna. 1966. *A Short History of Kerala.* Ernakulam, India: Pai.

Bayly, Susan. 1989. *Saints, Goddesses and Kings: Muslims and Christians in South Indian Society.* New York: Cambridge University Press.

Beck, Brenda, et al., eds. 1987. *Folktales of India.* Chicago: University of Chicago Press.

Blackburn, Stuart H. 1988. *Singing of Birth and Death: Texts in Performance.* Philadelphia: University of Pennsylvania Press.

Brown, C. P. 1986. *Verses of Vemana.* New Delhi: Asian Educational Services.

Chandran, Praphulla Satish. 1985. *Folk Tales of Karnataka.* New Delhi: Sterling.

Chettiar, S. M. L. Lakshmanan. 1980. *Folklore of Tamil Nadu.* Delhi: National Book Trust.

Chopra, P., T. K. Ravindran, and N. Subrahmanian. 1979. *History of South India.* New Delhi: S. Chand.

Choondal, Chummar. 1980. *Kerala Folk Literature.* Chettupuzha, India: Kerala Folklore Academy.

Cowell, E. B., ed. 1973. *The Jataka.* London: Pali Text Society, vols. 1–6.

Dehajia, Vidya. 1990. "On Modes of Visual Narration in Early Buddhist Art." *The Art Bulletin*, vol. LXXII, no. 3, 374–92.

Dharampal. 1971. *Indian Science and Technology in the Eighteenth Century.* Delhi: Impex India.

Dubey, Manjulika, and Brikram Grewal. 1990. *Insight Guides: South India.* Singapore: APA.

Gurumurthy, Preemila. 1994. *Kathakalaksepa.* Madras: International Society for the Investigation of Ancient Civilizations.

Hanur, Krishnamurthy, ed. 1991. *Encyclopedia of the Folk Culture of Karnataka.* Madras: Institute of Asian Studies.

James, Josef, ed. 1993. *Contemporary Indian Sculpture: The Madras Metaphor.* Delhi: Oxford University Press.

Kanigel, Robert. 1991. *The Man Who Knew Infinity.* New York: Scribner's.

Kassebaum, Gayathri. 1994. "Katha: Six Performance Traditions and the Preservation of Group Identity in Karnataka, South India." Seattle, WA: University of Washington. (Unpublished Ph.D. dissertation.)

Khorana, Meena. 1991. *The Indian Subcontinent in Literature for Children and Young Adults: An Annotated Bibliography of English Language Books.* Westport, CT: Greenwood Press.

Kingscote, H., and Pandit Natesa Sastri. 1890. *Tales of the Sun: Folklore of Southern India.* New York: Arno Press, repr. 1977.

MacDonald, Margaret Read. 1982. *The Storyteller's Sourcebook.* Detroit: Neal-Schuman/Gale.

Maharajan, S. 1979. *Tiruvalluvar.* New Delhi: Sahitya Akademi.

Mair, Victor H. 1988. *Painting and Performance.* Honolulu: University of Hawaii Press.

Mines, Mattison. 1994. *Public Faces, Private Voices: Community and Individuality in South India.* Berkeley, CA: University of California Press.

Munshi, K. M., and R. R. Diwakar. 1963. *Immortal Words.* Bombay: Bharatiya Vidya Bhavan.

Nair, Radha. 1976. *Legends of Kerala.* Bombay: IBH Publishing.

Narasimhan, Sakuntala. "On Women: Showcasing the South." *India News Network Digest.* Feb. 16, 1997, vol. 2, issue 1419. [Online]. Available via E-mail: india-L@indnet.org

Narayan, R. K. Many of his stories and novels give a flavor of South Indian life: *The Guide, Malgudi Days, The Painter of Signs, The Financial Expert,* to name just a few.

Nayak, H. M., and B. R. Gopal. 1990. *South Indian Studies.* Mysore, India: Geetha Book House.

Panikkar, Kavalam Narayana. 1991. *Folklore of Kerala.* Delhi: National Book Trust.

Pratham, Muni Sri Mahendra Kumarji. 1984. *Jaina Stories*. Translated by K. C. Lalwani. Calcutta: Arhat Prakashan.

Raghavan, V. 1979. *The Great Integrators: The Saint-Singers of India*. New Delhi: Ministry of Information and Broadcasting.

Rajagopalachari, C. 1971. *Avvaiar, The Great Tamil Poetess*. Bombay: Bharatiya Vidya Bhavan.

Rajamanickam, Mugavai. 1985. *Folk Tales of Tamil Nadu*. New Delhi: Ministry of Information and Broadcasting.

Rama Raju, B. 1981. *Folk Tales of Andhra Pradesh*. New Delhi: Sterling.

Ramakrishnan, G., N. Gayathri, and D. Chattophadhyaya, eds. 1983. *An Encyclopedia of South Indian Culture*. Calcutta: K. P. Bagchi.

Ramanujan, A. K., ed. 1991. *Folktales from India*. New York: Pantheon.

——, trans. 1985. *Poems of Love and War*. New York: Columbia University Press.

Richman, Paula. 1991. *Many Ramayanas*. Berkeley, CA: University of California Press.

Ryder, Arthur, trans. 1956. *The Panchatantra*. Chicago: University of Chicago Press.

Sastri, Nilakanta. 1987. *A History of South India*. Madras: Oxford University Press.

Seethalakshmi, K. A. 1986. *Folk Tales of Tamilnadu*. New Delhi: Sterling.

Shaikh, Munir. 1995. *Teaching About Islam and Muslims*. Fountain Valley, CA: Council on Islamic Education.

Sharma, V. S. 1982. *Thullal*. Madras: Higginbothams.

Shintri, Sarojini, and K. Raghavendra Rao.1983. *Women Freedom Fighters in Karnataka*. Dharwad, India: Prasaranga Karnatak University.

Shulman, David. 1985. *The King and the Clown in South Indian Myth and Poetry*. Princeton, NJ: Princeton University Press.

Spell of the South. 1987. Thanjavur: South Zone Cultural Centre.

Subramaniam, Kamala. 1980. *Mahabharata*. Bombay: Bharatiya Vidya Bhavan.

——. 1983. *Ramayana*. Bombay: Bharatiya Vidya Bhavan.

Tawney, C. H., trans. 1968. *Katha Sarit Sagara*. vols. 1-2. Delhi: Munshiram Manoharlal.

Thompson, Stith. 1955-1958. *Motif-Index of Folk Literature*. Bloomington, IN: Indiana University Press.

Vanmikanathan, G. 1985. *Periya Puranam*. Madras: Sri Ramakrishna Math.

Wadley, Susan S., ed. 1980. *The Powers of Tamil Women*. Syracuse, NY: Syracuse University, Maxwell School of Citizenship and Public Affairs. (South Asian Series, No. 6).

Welbon, Guy, and G. Yocum, eds. 1982. *Religious Festivals in South India and Sri Lanka*. New Delhi: Manohar.

Winters, Clyde Ahmed. 1992. "Megalithic Culture in South India." In *Dravidian Encyclopedia*, vol. 1, 453-55. Thiruvananthapuram: International School of Dravidian Linguistics.

For Children

Axworthy, Anni. 1992. *Anni's India Diary*. New York: Whispering Coyote Press.

DeRoin, Nancy. 1975. *Jataka Tales: Tales from the Buddha*. Boston: Houghton Mifflin.

Dhar, Sheila. 1973. *This India*. New Delhi: Government of India, Publications Division.

Easwaran, Eknath. *The Monkey and the Mango*. Tomales, CA: Nilgiri Press.

Ganeri, Anita. 1996. *Hindu*. New York: Childrens Press.

Gordon, Susan. 1990. *Asian Indians*. New York: Franklin Watts.

Hermes, Jules. 1993. *The Children of India*. Minneapolis: Carolrhoda Books.

Jaffrey, Madhur. 1985. *Seasons of Splendour*. New York: Atheneum.

Kadodwala, Dilip. 1995. *Hinduism*. New York: Thomson Learning.

Khandpur, Swarn. 1994. *Tell Me More About India*. New Delhi: India Book House.

Lal, Lakshmi. 1988. *The Ramayana*. Delhi: Orient Longman.

Nilakanta, Leela. 1973. *Tales From A South Indian Village*. New Delhi: Children's Book Trust.

Rauf, Abdur. 1990. *Stories from Prophet's Life*. Lahore, India: Ferozsons.

Thematic Index

Loyalty rewarded
 "The Loyal Parrot," 86

Modern jokes
 "The Making of a Sword," 130
 "One Sad Story," 128
 "The Shy Soldier," 129
 "Thin Milk," 130

Peasant as hero
 "Obavva of the Pestle," 112–13
Piety rewarded
 "Worship of Great and Small,"
  55–56
Pride is punished
 "Great Wealth, Great Pride,"
  48–50
Profitable exchange
 "Mouse Merchant," 95–97
Prophecy
 "Telling the Future," 69–70

Respect for family and elders
 "A Devoted Son," 73–74
 "My Son, Your Son," 78
 "Strange Fruit," 75–77
 "A Teacher's Skill," 79–80
 "Who Will Win," 72

Reward (boon) received
 "The Great Battle," 61–62
 "The Loyal Parrot," 86
Reward by deity
 "The Squirrel's Stripes," 100
Reward for faith
 "Druva," 57–60
 "Krishna and Sudama," 89–90
Reward for industry
 "The Guru," 98–99
 "Mouse Merchant," 95–97

Self sacrifice
 "The Elephant King," 102–5
Simplicity
 "Serving with Care," 42
Tricksters and tricks
 "The Fish Curry," 124–25
 "Golden Mangoes," 122
 "A Queenly Yawn," 120–21
 "A Real Bargain," 123
 "Sweet Sorrow," 121

Wit and humor. *See* Fools; Modern
 jokes; Tricksters and tricks

Index

"Fig" after page number denotes a figure; "pho" denotes a photograph.

Bhima
   "Soma and Bhima," 46–47
   "A Tale of Dharma," 63–65
Bible stories, 52
Bijapur dynasty, 5
Blackburn, Stuart H., 33, 36
Borwein, Peter, 116
Brahman, 14
   "The Great Battle," 61–62
Brahmin, 139
British rule, 6–7, 101, 114
Brown, C. P., 16
Buddha
   "The Elephant King," 102–5
Buddhism, 13
   former centers in Andhra Pradesh,
      10
   The Jataka tale, 102, 147,
      148–49
   and use of paintings, 36
Burra Katha storytelling style,
    26–27, 26(pho)
   and dialogue and questions, 36

Captain
   "The Greedy Guest," 43–45
Captain's wife
   "The Greedy Guest," 43–45
Caste system, 13, 15–16, 101
   and festivals, 131, 132
   improvement of conditions, 7
   subject of songs, 33
   "A Teacher's Skill," 79–80
Chakyar Kuttu storytelling style, 27
   insults element, 35
   and study of Sanskrit, 32
Chakyar, Mani Madhavar, 32
Chase, Richard, 144
Chera dynasty, 12
Chettiar, S. M. L. Lakshmanan, 131
Chidambaram Pillai, V. O., 7
Children, 31, 32, 71
Chistianity, 12, 13
Chitra Katha (picture story), 37–38,
    37(pho)

Chola dynasty, 4, 9
Clothing, 23
Coinage, 4, 23
Communism, 11, 26, 27
Contemporary Indian Sculpture:
    The Madras Metaphor, 19
Cowell, E. B., 147
   "Cullaka-Setthi Jataka," 148
   The Jataka, 147
   "Mahasuka Jataka," 147
Crocodile Bank, 9
"Cullaka-Setthi Jataka," 148
Cultural characteristics, 2–3

Daily life, 20–24
Dance, 16–17
Darika, 61
   "The Great Battle," 61–62
Dasaratha
   "A Devoted Son," 73–74
de Gama, Vasco, 6
Deccan plateau, 2
Dehajia, Vidya, 149
Devas
   "The Great Battle," 61–62
Devotees, 51
   "Druva," 57–60
Devotional songs, 33
Dhar, Sheila, 101
Dharampal, 6, 12, 19
Dharma, 63
   "A Tale of Dharma," 63–65
Dhoti, 23
Dialogue, 36
Diwakar, R. R., 51
Doctor
   "The Greedy Guest," 43–45
Doll
   "Yes Dear, Do," 82–85
Donkey
   "Strange Fruit," 75–77
Draupadi
   "A Tale of Dharma,"
      63–65
Dravidian people, 2–3, 11
Drought, 7

163

About the Authors

Cathy Spagnoli

Once an American storyteller traveled overland to India, had many adventures, and met a fine young sculptor. She returned home, finished college, and sold the sculptor's batiks for an air ticket. After two and a half years, the sculptor flew to Boston on 7/7/77—a lucky day. Soon after, they married and returned to live in Cholamandal, a lovely artists' colony south of Chennai, for two years. Then they moved to Seattle, and in 1986 welcomed their marvelous son, Manu. The three live now in a house that they built by themselves (with much help from family) on Vashon Island near Seattle. There in the woods, they eat chicken biryani and masala dosa while they plan their next visit to India.

Cathy, the storyteller, and Paramasivam, the sculptor, also keep busy with their work. Paramasivam has been a professional artist since 1968, working both in his native India and in the United States. He has received awards from various government bodies in India and exhibited in

Paramasivam Samanna

numerous shows. His works are in collections in the United States, Canada, Europe, Japan, and India. He has received funding for arts education projects from King County and Seattle Arts Commissions, as well as from the Seattle Art Museum.

Cathy has been a professional storyteller for 20 years. She has spent more than 10 years collecting tales and sharing stories across Asia, supported by The Japan Foundation, The Korea Foundation, United States Information Agency, and regional institutions. She gives storytelling performances and workshops regularly in Asia, the United States, and Canada. Cathy has written a number of children's books, including the ALA Notable *Nine-in-One, Grr! Grr!* (San Francisco: Children's Book Press), and has made several cassette tapes of Asian tales.

Manu loves travel, snowboarding, and stories. He is proud to be Indian and likes to eat Indian food with his fingers. Visit the whole family on their web page: www.nwlink.com/~spagnoli/

Paramasivam, Manu, and Cathy.